The Veteran Hiring Leader's ★★Handbook★★

Peter A. Gudmundsson

President and Chief Executive Officer
RecruitMilitary, LLC

RECRUIT///ILITARY®

RecruitMilitary, LLC
422 West Loveland Avenue
Loveland, OH 45140
www.recruitmilitary.com

Printed in the United States of America

First Edition

First Printing, 2016

For America's
military veterans
and those smart enough
to hire them

"It is the soldier, not the reporter,
who has given us freedom of the press.
It is the soldier, not the poet,
who has given us freedom of speech.
It is the soldier, not the organizer,
who gave us the freedom to demonstrate.
It is the soldier who salutes the flag,
who serves beneath the flag,
and whose coffin is draped by the flag,
who allows the protester to burn the flag."

Father Dennis Edward O'Brien, USMC

Contents

Section I
Why Hire Veterans?

Section II
Understanding Our Veterans

Section III
How to Hire Veterans

Section IV
The Veteran's Perspective

Appendix

Preface

When I became the President and CEO of Recruit-Military in 2013, I took charge of a company that was already an industry leader and doing great work at helping organizations hire veterans. Since the beginning, my goal has been to turn RecruitMilitary into both a nationwide military recruiting powerhouse and also a thought-leader on veteran hiring issues.

Putting veterans to work is popular media fodder these days. Supporting our troops is "in." Yellow ribbons abound on car bumpers and highway overpasses across the country. While supporting those who defend and fight for our country is important and the right thing to do, a strong argument can be made that the cultural push to rally around veterans and thank them for their service has reduced what was once heartfelt patriotism to white noise – something that we tune out and largely ignore.

Yet, at the same time that we, as a country, conduct a sort of "hero worship" for those who have served, we also seem to have the mentality that these "heroes" are victims – especially when it comes to the job market.

The idea that veterans should be hired because the public feels sorry for them may be well-intentioned, but is ultimately harmful. Often the sentiment is based on incorrect data. For example, it is widely believed that veterans suffer from more unemployment than regular citizens when the fact is the opposite, according to the Bureau of Labor Statistics. Veterans are actually more employed because they are in fact better at getting work done!

Unfortunately, too many veteran service organizations and government programs are rooted in the notion that veterans have a harder time getting on with their civilian careers and need special help. This can lead to a noxious combination of entitlement, self-pity, and defeatism on behalf of otherwise well-qualified individuals.

It is high time to turn that rhetoric on its ear. All too often, organizations seeking to help veterans get jobs focus on guilt or entitlement. This is the wrong approach. Rather, the focus should be on the employer and the demand side: Employers need great people. Companies like RecruitMilitary can help organizations find them. By acting as "fishing guides" who lead organizations to pools of talent, we can help employers hire, appreciate, and retain our nation's very best: our military veterans.

Why hire veterans? Military experience offers discipline and training that creates solid, effective leaders who go on to become motivated and successful employees. The bottom line is that hiring veterans is not charity work – it's simply good business.

Of course, because you are reading this handbook, chances are you have just been assigned to some aspect of your company's veteran hiring initiative. No doubt, you have many other responsibilities that demand your time in other aspects of talent acquisition – general operations, diversity and inclusion, regulatory compliance, or general human resources. You may or may not have served yourself or known someone well who is a veteran. You have questions. The good news is that this handbook has your answers.

By hiring veterans, employers have a chance to get it right from the start. There is a better way to hire, and the business sectors need to lead by example. This manual will illustrate just a few of the many reasons that military veterans make good civilian hires, and show the organizational executive the actual "how to" of assembling a veteran hiring effort that will be effective and economical.

Thank you for your service to America's best talent.

Peter A. Gudmundsson
Loveland, Ohio and Dallas, Texas
2016

Section I
Why Hire Veterans?

Introduction
Why Hire Veterans?

The foundational reason for hiring veterans is a matter of simple logic:

- All organizations need to hire great people.
- Veterans are great people.
- Therefore, all organizations need to hire veterans.

Hiring veterans just makes good business sense. As one veteran hiring leader told me, "Don't hire veterans because you feel sorry for them. Hire them because they are the most qualified people around."

Another hiring professional calls veterans "Leaders in a box," remarking, "They fit just about everywhere. Most are college-educated, many served under strenuous circumstances, saw combat action, and can use resources well."

Intangible Characteristics

Transitioning and veteran military have characteristics that make them great civilian employees, including leadership, initiative, self-discipline, teamwork, and an excellent work ethic. Tapping this pool of skilled, disciplined, and hardworking talent is the logical step for any employer that wants to "work smart."

Smart employers know that veterans
- work efficiently within an organizational system
- have already been through rigorous training and completed it satisfactorily
- can deal with people and numbers under pressure
- are well-versed in small unit leadership at an early stage of their careers, giving them more experience and maturity than their civilian counterparts of the same age
- have, in many cases, experienced combat
− how much more stressful can your business be?

Specific Skills

Typical transitioning personnel do not need industry experience to make a positive impact in the workplace immediately. They acquired outstanding skills and training while in the service. The overwhelming majority of active-duty personnel work in military employment categories that have easily recognized civilian counterparts, ranging from "Engineering, Science, and Technical" and "Machine Operator and Precision Work" to "Executive, Administrative, and Managerial." Personnel who trained in combat occupations make great leaders in Corporate America.

In addition, a high proportion of veterans have the security clearances necessary for certain civilian jobs. Clearances are especially valuable to companies that hold or seek federal contracts.

Compliance

Veterans can help employers meet diversity goals. Active-duty personnel are:[1]

- 20% African-American
- 9% Hispanic
- 15% women.

In addition, a Final Rule from the Office of Federal Contract Compliance Programs (OFCCP), a part of the U.S. Department of Labor, became effective on March 24, 2014, affecting the hiring and employment of veterans. It requires federal contractors and subcontractors to take affirmative action to recruit, hire, promote, and retain veterans that fall into certain groups. Benchmarks for hiring must be met, based on various national percentages of veterans in the labor force and on data from the Bureau of Labor Statistics (BLS) and the Veterans' Employment and Training Service/Employment and Training Administration (VETS/ETA).

Contractors that hire veterans as their go-to source for filling positions will find that they are already ahead of the game.

---

[1]

http://download.militaryonesource.mil/12038/MOS/Reports/2014-Demographics-Report.pdf

Low Cost per Hire

In today's business climate, time is money. When it is vital to find top talent quickly, as well as to attract and retain the right people, companies will save time and money if they set out to hire veterans from the get-go.

Why? Their intangible characteristics result in a shorter learning curve, even if a veteran is placed in an unfamiliar role. Furthermore, military-to-civilian recruitment firms such as RecruitMilitary can make the selection process go faster because they offer access to a large and diverse pool of veteran talent at once – the sourcing equivalent of "one-stop shopping." These firms provide access to veterans in a variety of ways, including career fairs, database searches, email and newsletter targeting, and searching by on-site recruiters filling specific job orders.

Because the training provided in the military is universal, it gives all soldiers the same common ground. One veteran remarked, "I don't need to know everyone in the military, because we all have the same foundation."

Additionally, the tax breaks that have been available to companies that hire veterans further add to the bottom line, making veterans cost-effective hires.

Public Relations Benefits

Many companies want to be perceived as veteran-friendly employers, regardless of whether they plan to implement a veteran hiring program. As one employer noted in a study on veteran hiring conducted by the Center for a New American Security, "We think it's good to associate our brand with the military brand, which is our country's most trusted institution. It's good for our brand's reputation."

Gratitude for Service

I have left for last the reason that is often cited first in commentary on military-to-civilian recruitment: Hire veterans as a way of giving them a helping hand to re-pay them for their service and sacrifice. One HR director put it this way: "We are an American company, and hiring veterans is the right thing to do."

*"As we express our gratitude,
we must never forget
that the highest appreciation
is not to utter words,
but to live by them."*

John F. Kennedy

Chapter 1
Intangible Characteristics

There are few institutions that select for and teach the intangible skills and attitudes that define the successful. Most veterans were initially drawn to service because they wanted to be part of something bigger than themselves and wanted to give back. True, they may actually have joined for tangible benefits such as education or adventure. But beneath those personal goals there typically lies an element of service.

So it is that hiring people of character is one of the primary benefits of selecting employees from the pool of veterans. Imagine that you lived in a medieval village and a messenger arrived to declare that a raiding party was nearby – and that volunteers were needed to deter and defeat the force. Who would volunteer to meet that challenge? Certainly not everyone. Only those who valued the community over their own selfish purposes would repond. Today, those people are our military personnel and our veterans.

Trained to Lead

Military culture emphasizes leadership and teamwork. Not all veterans are great leaders, but virtually all of them have been exposed to the aspirational ideals of leadership – and they at least know how one should try to lead others. This is not true for former officers alone. Even at the most basic level of enlisted training, privates and seamen apprentice are exposed to the ways of taking charge and getting things done.

Organizationally Adept

Veterans already know how to navigate organizations. They know when to follow procedures and when and how to circumvent bureaucracies to accomplish the unit's larger mission. This sort of collective and individual organizational emotional intelligence is vital for teams of all sizes in Corporate America.

Already Screened

Only 30% of young Americans could even qualify for military service.[2] So, when you hire veterans, you are already starting at the seventieth percentile of American youth. Drug use, lack of physical fitness, failure to finish high school, and excessive tattoos or piercings are all reasons why people fail to qualify. Is that the employee base you want for your company?

2

http://time.com/2938158/youth-fail-to-qualify-military-service/

Mission First

Veterans are attracted to organizations with understandable missions, and veterans themselves tend to be selfless and team-oriented. What civilian team or group would not want to staff itself with individuals who instinctively and consciously subordinate their egos to accomplish tasks and meet strategic goals?

Beyond Command and Control

An unfortunate stereotype of military culture is that a command-and-control hierarchy prevails or even dominates. Yes, it is true that following orders is both culturally and legally necessary for military success. However, in actual practice, modern warfare and combat support thrive on decentralized decision-making as much as, or more than, modern corporate operations. Especially in the ground forces, the Army and Marine Corps, individual servicemembers need to process information and make decisions in a rapidly changing environment. That same discipline and decisiveness can be harnessed for the success of your organization.

Integrity and Character

Basic Combat Training is incredibly stressful. It has to be in order to properly prepare individuals for war. This environment of intense pressure creates intense cultural emphasis on integrity and character, traits which are tested and solidified later, on the battlefield.

This is not to claim that veterans have a lock on integrity. It is rather to point out that they have an exposure and vocabulary that tends to focus them on the right and wrong ways to behave in shifting scenarios. Having been trained in matters of life and death, it is easier for veterans to fathom and process less complex issues of morality in a corporate operations context.

"The men and women of our military, their spouses and their families are some of the most gifted, talented employees that we have in the company."

**Lou D'Ambrosio
CEO, Sears Holdings**

Chapter 2
Specific Skills

In addition to intangible skills, the military is adept at training for specific skills. If one contemplates the near-miracle of taking a 17-year-old out of a local mall and turning him or her into an F-18 jet mechanic in less than a year, it makes sense that our military is enabled and willing to transfer complex skill sets.

Directly Transferable

In addition to softer specific skills, such as project and team management, the military is very good at teaching technical skills. Some of these skills are directly transferable to the civilian world. Among them are:

- Construction
- Information systems
- Law enforcement
- Piloting aircraft, spacecraft, and ships
- Driving
- Heavy equipment operation
- Payroll
- Law practice (lawyers, clerks, paralegals)
- Administration and human resources
- Logistics, transportation, and warehousing
- Medical and dental professions
- Food service

One can think of the military as a large vertically integrated corporation. Just about all the professions one can imagine are represented.

Indirectly Transferable

Some military-taught skills do not have direct parallels in the civilian world, but are very close when one breaks down the key tasks or responsibilities.

For example, field artillery is a combat arm that fires projectiles at targets that are many miles from the guns or launchers. There is no direct civilian use for the knowledge of how to acquire and locate targets, calculate firing data, and correctly fire weapons. On the other hand, countless organizations need people who can deal with numbers accurately while under intense pressure.

One challenge – and opportunity – with veteran talent is that even the potential employees themselves do not know how their skills relate to the civilian world. Some understand intuitively, but their humility or inexperience prevents them from articulating this value in a manner that makes sense to civilians.

*"Well, look at what people are doing
for returned veterans now. The wounded warriors.
They're working hard to make
the wounded veterans feel that they are loved
and welcomed home, unlike Vietnam.
It was not a very kind, gentle world then.
I think we are kinder and gentler."*

Barbara Bush

Chapter 3
Compliance

com·pli·ance [kuhm-plahy-uhns] noun
the act of conforming, acquiescing,
or yielding; cooperation or obedience.[3]

This definition can imply a "(heavy sigh)... it's because I have to, but I don't really want to" type of obligation or task. But at its core, compliance is really about ethics and the notion that every organization should strive to establish and maintain acceptable standards of behavior.

The Private Sector

The means by which companies implement this notion vary widely. They include:
- codes of conduct
- communicating policies that outline expected behaviors
- risk assessment tools
- incident reporting and management systems
- preventive and corrective action plans
- ongoing communication and outreach efforts to enforce standards

---

3

http://dictionary.reference.com/browse/compliance?s=t

Compliance policies protect companies and employees from unethical behavior, detect misconduct when it occurs, and prevent it from happening again. They also help shape a company's culture. Many firms outsource this function to entities that specialize in organizational compliance and ethics. Non-profit think tanks and organizations also exist to help employers and to share best practices.

Where Veterans Fit

Veteran hiring initiatives are not compliance per se, but a worthwhile goal.

Many businesses do not disclose publicly whether they have internal hiring goals or guidelines for hiring veterans. However, veteran hiring initiatives are on the rise. Many employers have launched specific veteran hiring campaigns as well as internal support networks and programs for the veterans who are already on their teams.

Some companies filter job applications and resumes that arrive at the "careers" or "opportunities" sections of their websites to find veterans, and then make a special effort to interview and hire veteran applicants.

Other companies have a web page for veterans in their careers sections, or even maintain military-specific sections. Some purchase recruitment advertising that targets veterans, and may attend a small number of job fairs on military bases or U.S. Chamber Hiring Our Heroes events. Companies may also post jobs for veterans on job boards that do not specialize in veteran outreach.

Other practices to bolster veteran hires:
- partnering with business and trade associations
- having veteran employees disseminate employment information to their personal networks
- involvement in the Army PaYS Program (Partnership for Youth Success) – strategic partnerships with the Army and various corporations, companies, and public sector agencies
- participating in Wounded Warriors live chats
- LinkedIn memberships and searches
- industry-focused veteran initiatives
- attending career centers at colleges
- attending veteran-focused career fairs
- participating in virtual career fairs
- contingency recruiting

Legal Compliance

On November 1, 1991, the United States Sentencing Commission (USSC) put into effect the Federal Sentencing Guidelines for Organizations (FSGO). Under the FSGO, organizations with ethics and compliance programs that meet defined standards earn credit toward reduced penalties if employees engage in wrongdoing – but organizations with substandard programs receive far tougher penalties.[4]

4

http://www.ethics.org/fsgo

Reservists and National Guard members who have been called to active duty have rights and responsibilities under the Uniformed Services Employment and Reemployment Rights Act (USERRA).

The Department of Labor's Office of Federal Contract Compliance Programs (OFCCP) promotes equal employment opportunity on behalf of qualified special disabled veterans, Vietnam era veterans, recently separated veterans, and veterans who served on active duty during a war or in a campaign or expedition for which a campaign badge has been authorized.[5]

Office of Federal Contract Compliance Program and Veterans
Federal contractors and subcontractors for the first time must adopt quantifiable hiring benchmarks for military veterans, including disabled veterans.

The purpose of the OFCCP is to enforce, for the benefit of job seekers and wage earners, the contractual promise of affirmative action and equal employment opportunity required of those who do business with the Federal government.

The Veterans Rule applies to federal contractors and covered subcontractors with a contract of $100,000 or more. Contractors and covered subcontractors with a

---

5

http://www.dol.gov/dol/topic/hiring/veterans.htm

contract of $100,000 or more and 50 or more employees must comply with the affirmative action plan requirements. The Final Rules became effective on March 24, 2014. [6]

However, the OFCCP made it clear that these benchmarks were not considered quotas, and failure to meet them would not be considered a violation of the Final Rules. Furthermore, the OFCCP did not anticipate that contractors would meet the benchmark or utilization goal in the first year after the Final Rules went into effect. Nevertheless, contractors must undertake positive outreach and recruitment efforts to reach veterans and must document those efforts, in turn.[7]

Bottom Line

All organizations need high-quality members, employees, partners, and associates. The general skills, attributes, and values of our veterans make them people of the highest quality. Veterans offer specific skills and experience (e.g., jet engine mechanic or team leader) that can be of immediate use and value to civilian organizations. As with any hiring policy, there exist best practices for excellence in veteran hiring. If followed, those practices will deliver measurable benefits to organizations.

6

http://www.cooley.com/unpacking-OFCCPs-final-rules-for-veterans-and-individuals-with-disabilities

7

Ibid.

*"If you can work with sophisticated radar that guide
high-speed missiles into outer space,
if you can operate complex communications systems
from a tent in a desert, then clearly,
you're ready to succeed in our high-tech industries
here at home.*

*If you can work with people
from all different cultures and backgrounds,
if you can lead dozens, even hundreds of your peers
in life-or-death missions, then clearly,
you've got the management and interpersonal skills
that we need in every sector of this economy."*

Michelle Obama

Chapter 4
Public Relations Benefits

A well-run veteran hiring initiative will be additive both to a general organization brand and a specific effort focused on an employee brand.

When a company communicates intelligently and clearly that it is interested in hiring veterans, it informs the market that it understands excellence, quality, and standards. The military is one of only a few institutions left in American society that is respected almost universally. According to Gallup, 72% of Americans hold the military in high regard.[8] An organization that is sincerely dedicated to hiring veterans will share in a portion of that esteem.

It is a sad reality that some organizations and individuals are more interested to be seen hiring veterans than actually leveraging the benefits of superior talent.

The eighteenth century English essayist Samuel Johnson wrote that "patriotism is the last refuge of a scoundrel." To which specific form of false patriotism Dr. Johnson was referring is unclear, but his meaning is apposite today.

---

[8]

http://www.gallup.com/poll/183593/confidence-institutions-below-historical-norms.aspx

---

Some observe that, within the military and veteran experience, there curiously co-exist measures of extreme cynicism and sincere idealism. This is a peculiar duality, but one that informs thoughtful publicity efforts around veteran hiring.

Good will and good intentions are the starting point – but not the end – of long-lasting veteran hiring success. Too many organizations do not perform the arduous task of explaining to their constituents exactly why they are interested in hiring veterans. Without a clear "why," it is difficult to generate interest in the "who" or "what."

Essential Facts

Furthermore, it is critical that any publicity effort communicates to the marketplace a few essential facts in order to be credible. Failure to convey those facts can produce a reaction opposite of what was intended.

The facts:
- Veterans are not victims. They do not need or deserve special treatment or handouts. Yes, some veterans may require reasonable accommodation for their physical or other limitations, but these are small concessions to gain the benefit of first-class talent.
- A positive orientation leads to better hiring decisions. Ask "how can this veteran help us?" rather than "what can go wrong with this veteran candidate?"
- Humility is important. Veteran culture does not tolerate show-offs. An organization must be humble in

its communications.

- The only one that receives a favor when a veteran is hired is the employer – for getting great talent.

Pitching a Story

When you pitch a veteran story to the media, keep in mind that there are unspoken rules around the accepted narratives concerning veterans. Most members of the media are not even aware that they have such narrow views, but being mindful of them will increase the chances that you will get a story placed.

These narratives fall into one of the following categories:
- Veterans are all messed up, and they deserve our fear, pity, or scorn.
- The community is rallying to thank and support veterans.
- The veteran next door is a great success, maybe even a surprisingly great success.
- Veterans are getting screwed by the Veterans Administration, shady businesses, or their own good intentions.
- Veterans are continuing to serve because that is what they do (includes hero stories).

If you conform your story pitch to one or more of these narratives, you increase your chance of getting placement. But, as mentioned earlier, while falling into one of these narratives may generate publicity for your organization, it is harmful to the job-seeking veteran community and to the American public.

"...It is a proud privilege to be a soldier –
a good soldier ... [with] discipline, self-respect,
pride in his unit and his country,
a high sense of duty and obligation
to comrades and to his superiors,
and a self-confidence
born of demonstrated ability."

George S. Patton, Jr.

Section II
Understanding
Our Veterans

Chapter 5
Today's Military

With fewer than 6% of American workers having served in the military, it is not at all surprising that direct knowledge of the military experience is generally lacking in our private economy. By contrast, in an earlier generation just about everyone had either served or knew someone who had.

The Services

Since the draft ended in 1975, our military has been an all-volunteer force. So which service a veteran initially selected tells you something about that individual's decision-making – at least when he or she was 18 to 22 years old.

The United States supports five military services, four of which are part of the Department of Defense and one of which, the Coast Guard, is part of the Department of Homeland Security. Each has a distinct mission and set of responsibilities, but there is some overlap.

What follows is a high-level overview of the services intended for civilians who are not experienced with the military. For the sake of brevity and usefulness, I have made certain generalizations. Any offense of commission or omission is unintended.

Reserve vs Active

Civilians are often confused by the terms Reserve, National Guard, and Active.

The experience of World War II, when the number of U.S. military personnel grew from 334 thousand in 1939 to 12 million in 1945 taught the nation never to be caught flat footed again. Because a junior soldier or officer can be trained quickly, but a midlevel or senior leader takes years to develop, the reserve forces contain part-time soldiers, sailors, airmen, and Marines who typically train one weekend per month and two weeks per year. They may be "called up" or mobilized for periods lasting for months or years. In addition, reserve forces are less expensive to maintain because the members presumably support themselves economically and are paid by the government only while training or activated.

The Army National Guard and the Air National Guard are, respectively, the Army and Air Force of each state. They report to the governor of their state, however, they can be "federalized" and become part of the national military by presidential order.

So, a reservist or guardsman can be called to active service and serve full-time even though he or she is a reservist.

Some states like California, Texas, and New York

also maintain State Guards. These volunteer forces focus their efforts on in-state disaster response and civil defense. State Guard forces cannot be "federalized" and rarely deploy for more than a few days at a time.

The United States Army

The oldest and largest service, the Army fights the nation's land wars. With 475,000 active and 540,000 National Guard and Army Reserve forces, the Army recruits about sixty thousand new soldiers each year, training them to do everything from combat arms (e.g., infantry, special forces, tank operation, combat engineering, air defense artillery, field artillery), logistics, supply, transportation, military police, intelligence, and helicopter aviation.

Only about 20% of Army personnel are "trigger pulling" combat arms "war fighters." Many more serve in support roles that enable the fighters to do their jobs.

Army cultural loyalties are strongest at the unit level. Their uniforms display colorful unit badges and distinctive headgear such as berets or cavalry hats to express their belonging. Places like the United

States Military Academy (West Point) and Ranger School strongly emphasize leadership and management training. Because of this emphasis and the fluid nature of modern land combat, Army veterans often excel in small team roles where judgment and discretion are critical.

When an employer thinks of modern Army veterans, he or she should think problem-solving in real time in order to accomplish missions under stress in constantly changing environments. The employer should not conjure up the World War I stereotype of robotic soldiers blindly following suicidal orders to leave their trenches to be mowed down by enemy machine guns.

The United States Air Force

The newest of the services, the U.S. Air Force (USAF) was formed in 1947, when the Army Air Corps broke off from its parent service. The Air Force has both strategic and tactical aspects. The former involves maintaining the deterrent forces of nuclear intercontinental ballistic missiles (ICBM's), large bombers, and satellites. The latter involves fighter aircraft that support ground operations and attack targets on a more regional scale.

Because it is a newer branch, the Air Force often has better amenities and base locations. Other services tease the Air Force airmen for having the cushiest lifestyles due to their higher quality living quarters and golf courses. Probably the most "relaxed" of the services from a strict "yes sir/no sir" perspective, the Air Force is nevertheless very strict on procedures and protocols. One does not just "wing it" (pun intended) where nuclear weapons and complex systems are concerned. In addition, the Air Force tends to be rather stringent in their recruiting standards, resulting in a highly intelligent service, capable of high-level critical thinking.

The Air Force is also known for its state-of-the-art technical training.

The United States Marine Corps

The Marine Corps is simply the Navy's own personal army. It exists to project power from the sea. Because of this difficult mission, it has adopted an elite and aggressive style that attracts young men and women who both desire a challenge and wish to join what is essentially an intensely positive cult. Marine advertising clearly delineates the brand promise of service as a Marine:

"Maybe You Can Be One of Us."
"The Few, The Proud, The Marines."
"We Never Promised You a Rose Garden."

Mission accomplishment at any ethical cost is the hallmark of the Marines, and USMC veterans typically display an enthusiasm for challenge and achievement that some other veterans both admire and condemn as excessive.

The Marines have their own air force of planes and helicopters, and they deploy sophisticated technology. But at the end of the day, Marine veterans are known for small unit leadership, adaptable operating styles, and dogged determination.

Important to note: Marines do not use the phrase "former Marine." The terms "Marine veteran" and "retired Marine" are preferred.

The United States Navy

"Join the Navy and See the World" has been the recruiting mantra of the Navy since the days of sailing ships. A highly diverse service, the Navy includes surface ships, submarines, fixed and rotary aircraft, small river patrol boats, special commando forces (SEALs), and a detailed logistical train.

Most Navy jobs are very technical in nature. Ships are essentially floating factories, so sailors learn maintenance and industrial engineering skills that translate easily to commercial applications.

Full of tradition and ceremony, the Navy produces veterans who are fiercely loyal to their ships and squadrons. They understand metrics and quality standards intuitively, and they will intuitively blend industrial and human factors to achieve excellence.

The United States Coast Guard

The smallest of the five services, the Coast Guard employs only 40,000 active Coast Guardsmen and women. One can think of the USCG as a hybrid of a small navy, a police force, and a fire department. The Coast Guard deploys in small ships, boats, and aircraft to perform different missions including law enforcement, maritime security, search and rescue, and environmental protection.

"Coasties" are resourceful people because they are notoriously under-budgeted, self-effacing, and flexible. They have little time or patience for military spit-and-polish because they are so busy with their diverse missions. In addition, Coast Guard veterans are more used to working and living among civilians because most of their bases are small and integrated at the community level.

Rank and Seniority

Officers

The structure of the military ranks often perplexes civilians. The Constitution gives the president the power to command the armed forces. Obviously, the president is too busy to take personal charge of all activities, so he issues commissions to individuals to serve in command and staff positions in his place. These men and women are called commissioned officers. In civilian terms, officers are much like executives and middle managers.

Officers receive commissions from three major sources:
- Service academies such as the United States Military Academy at West Point for the Army, the Naval Academy in Annapolis, the Air Force Academy near Colorado Springs, and the Coast Guard Academy, which is in New London, Connecticut. One-sixth of Naval Academy graduates become Marine officers.
- Reserve Officer Training Corps (ROTC) at selected college and universities. College students study military subjects in addition to their regular studies.
- Officer Candidate School (OCS), which is like boot camp for officers. Some are highly selective – such as the Marine Corps Officer Candidates School at Quantico, Virginia. Often, fewer than 50% of the candidates do not finish the program. Virtually all OCS's require a bachelor's degree.

In most of the services, enlisted personnel can attend OCS and then become officers.

Warrant Officers
In each service, there is a track for skilled personnel to become warrant officers. Most have technical expertise – think Scotty from the original Star Trek.

On the military seniority table, the warrant officers are ranked between the most junior commissioned officer and the most senior enlisted person. They are generally respected by all because of the technical insight and experience they offer.

The Army names some personnel as warrant officers after they finish their initial training – most notably, helicopter pilots.

Enlisted Personnel
Over 84% of military personnel (and therefore veterans) are or were enlisted. These are the men and women who do the "real" work every day. These days, virtually all of them have at least a high school education and many have a few semesters of college.

Enlisted Ranks

=== ★ ★ ★ ===

E-1 through E-3

- Great development talent for junior roles.
- The "doers," working well in teams to accomplish daily missions.
- May include roles such as maintenance technician, network administrator, or driver.

E-4

- Make great supervisors for teams of 3-8 individuals.
- A few more years experience and maturity.
- Maturity and technical competence make them excellent choice for field service or route-sales type roles.

E-5

- Typically have completed multiple enlistments and attended leadership schools.
- Junior leaders perform well in teams of 10-12 members.
- High-energy individuals perform well in sales roles.

E-6

- Typically have served 10-15 years.
- Leadership role with teams of 7-15.
- May be key members on operational staffs with specialized skills.
- Have great impact in individual contributor technical roles or first-line leadership roles.

E-7

- Typically have served 12-20 years.
- Leadership role with teams of 15-40.
- Proven effective in production supervisor, site manager, and maintenance leadership roles across variety of industries.
- Strong individual contributors in key positions such as sales roles.

E-8

- Typically served 20+ years.
- Have served at more strategic level, but also excellent at driving tactical results.
- Leadership of groups ranging from hundreds to thousands.
- Well suited for key leader roles, consultative specialty roles.

Officer Ranks

== * ★ * ==

0-1 through 0-3

- Known collectively as former junior military officers, or JMO's.
- Have served from 3 to 10 years in tactical leadership roles.
- Typically suited for civilian roles as operations supervisors, territory managers, process engineers, and other mid-level leaders.

0-4

- Typically have served 10-15 years, or 20 years if they were enlisted personnel before becoming officers.
- In addition to tactical leadership experience, have gained significant staff / planning experience.
- Able to pick up specific industry knowledge quickly.
- Fit well into senior manager and director-level roles.

0-5 and 0-6

- Former senior officers that have served 20+ years at the highest levels of strategic leadership.
- Have led hundreds or thousands – or tens of thousands – of troops.
- Able to move into high-level executive positions in Corporate America.
- Employers in defense-related industries especially like such candidates because of their depth of experience.

Rank and Experience

What do ranks/rates tell employers regarding the suitability of candidates for various kinds of work? The summaries below are based on RecruitMilitary's 18+ years of experience in helping employers find outstanding veteran talent. The summaries apply especially well to transitioning military and to men and women who have been out of the service for up to five years or so. Employers should, of course, factor in the civilian work experience – and the educational advancement – of veterans who have been out of the service for a longer time.

E-1's through E-3's often provide great development talent in the most junior roles in a company. Because they are the "doers" in the service, they work well in teams to accomplish daily missions using their hands-on skills. These may include roles such as driver, maintenance technician, or network administrator.

E-4's often make great supervisors for teams of three to eight individuals. Additionally, with a few more years of experience under their belt, they have developed a level of maturity that, when combined with their technical competence, makes them an excellent choice for field-service or route-sales type roles.

E-5's bring a bit more practical and formal leadership training to the table. Typically, they have completed multiple enlistment periods in the service and they have attended the leadership schools each service operates. These junior leaders perform well in small team (around 10 to 20 members) leadership roles. And high-energy individuals at this level perform well in sales roles that require a rigorous level of activity and persistence.

E-6's typically have served between 10 and 15 years, and will excel in leadership roles with teams of 7 to 15. They may also be key members on operational staffs that have specialized individual skills. Over the years, RecruitMilitary has seen E-6's have great impact in individual contributor technical roles and team leader or first-line leadership roles.

E-7's are quintessential small-unit leaders with teams of 15 to 40 individuals, and they usually will have served between 12 and 20 years. These leaders have proven effective in production supervisor, site manager, and maintenance leadership roles across a variety of industries. Additionally, they are strong individual contributors in key positions such as sales roles.

E-8's and E-9's have a great breadth and depth of experience and typically have served 20+ years. Among the enlisted ranks/rates, these individuals have often served at a more strategic level, but yet have maintained an excellence at driving tactical results. They will have led organizations ranging from hundreds to thousands of servicemembers. Because of their diverse and deep experience, these candidates are well suited for key leader roles, consultative specialty roles, and other positions where strategic thinking and hands-on leadership will drive results.

O-1's through O-3's – known collectively as former junior military officers, or JMO's – have served from 3 to 10 years in tactical leadership roles. Those candidates find civilian homes as operations supervisors, territory managers, process engineers, and other mid-level leaders.

RecruitMilitary recognized the value of former JMO's early in our existence. We began in 1998 as a firm that placed former JMO's with companies throughout Corporate America on a contingency basis.

O-4's typically have served 10 to 15 years, or 20 years if they were enlisted personnel before becoming officers. In addition to tactical leadership experience, they have gained significant staff/planning experience. Furthermore, they are able to pick up specific industry knowledge quickly. With all those attributes, they fit well into senior manager and director-level roles.

O-5's and O-6's – former senior officers – have served 20+ years. They have performed at the highest levels of strategic leadership. They have led hundreds or thousands – or tens of thousands – of troops, so they can move into high-level executive positions in Corporate America. Employers in defense-related industries especially like such candidates because of their depth of experience.

*"The willingness with which our young people
are likely to serve in any war,
no matter how justified,
shall be directly proportional
to how they perceive
the Veterans of earlier wars were treated
and appreciated by their nation."*

George Washington

Chapter 6
Understanding Military Achievement [9]

When a mere 7.3% of the U.S. population has served in the armed forces, I am hardly surprised that many corporate recruiters and hiring managers are unsure, or at least unconfident, about how to assess a veteran job candidate.

I have found that the best way to evaluate a candidate, regardless of background, is to determine whether he or she:

- can do the work,
- is willing to do the work, and
- would be a cultural fit for your company.

Some call this a "can do, will do, and fit" assessment. Military veterans are like other candidates in this regard, but certain unique tips and tactics can help interviewers better evaluate veterans. I categorize these aids under headings I call the Three A's: Achievement, Attitude, and Ambition.

9

Portions of this chapter originally appeared as an article in *U.S. News & World Report* on October 1, 2015

http://money.usnews.com/money/blogs/outside-voices-careers/2015/10/01/how-to-assess-a-veteran-job-candidate

Achievement

Of the three, assessing individual military achievement flummoxes hiring decision-makers the most. As with other applicants – and unlike mutual funds – past performance is the best indication of future results. The challenge for the evaluator is to understand the nature of the candidate's achievements in the context of the military experience. Five categories of achievement should be reviewed:

1. Rank Advancement

Because the military is a large and often bureaucratic organization, many aspects of rank promotion are a function of "time-in-grade" guidelines. But in some services – the Navy for example – eligible enlisted personnel can show initiative by studying for and passing examinations for promotion. Therefore, it is a good idea to ask a veteran: "Tell me about your promotion history in the service. Were you promoted on track, or ahead of your peers?" Listen for responses that include phrases such as "meritorious promotion," "sat for the examination," etc.

Commissioned officer promotions tend to be more time-based, but one can ask: "What did your official evaluation reports say about your performance?" Each service has is own name for these reports, but all have them.

2. Awards

All military services love to issue badges, ribbons,

medals, and other awards.

- Some identify the holder as a genuine combat hero – e.g., Navy Cross, Silver Star.
- Some recognize generally administrative or garrison accomplishments – e.g., Army Achievement Medal.
- Others are given to units or individuals for participation in campaigns or deployments – e.g., Afghanistan Campaign Medal.
- Finally, there are some that are basically for showing up or staying out of trouble – e.g., Good Conduct and National Defense medals.

If you are unsure what decorations mean, and they are listed on a resume, ask a veteran to help you interpret, do some online research, or ask the applicant directly. Most veterans are very honest about the relative importance of certain awards, and will not be shy to share with you their true meaning.

Do not hold the absence of certain awards against a candidate. For example, a sergeant on a general's staff is more likely to have earned formal awards than a front-line squad leader. Seek to understand the context in which recognition is granted.

3. Military School Selection and Completion

More impressive than most decorations and awards are the many military schools that feature rigorous selection and completion criteria. Most hiring managers know that the service academies such as West Point are highly selective colleges, but how many know that only 42% of those who enter U.S. Army Ranger School complete its arduous nine-week course?

Likewise, schools from the Navy's Nuclear Propulsion and Underwater Demolition to the Air Force Para-Rescue and Marine Officer Candidates School routinely screen out large numbers of starting participants.

Again, for more information, ask colleagues who are veterans, do your online research, or ask the candidate himself about the courses he has completed.

4. Extracurricular Achievements
While on active duty, some servicemembers find time to complete civilian certifications and degrees, to perform community service, and even moonlight in jobs. One should be favorably impressed by personnel who accomplish these sorts of achievements, but slow to criticize those who do not. Training and deployment schedules and the nature of military life often conspire to make such activities impossible for those in highly challenging roles and units.

5. Civilian Achievements
A skilled interviewer will seek to understand the achievements and socialization that the candidate experienced before or after military service. Perhaps the veteran comes from a family of salespeople, assisted with a family retail store, or has worked in a local factory since leaving the service. Do not assume that a veteran has only uniformed experience. You may have

to tease this information out during an interview, but what you discover may come as a pleasant surprise.

Attitude

One area in which veterans typically shine is attitude. Teamwork, leadership, and mission orientation are almost certainties with most veteran candidates. But a skilled interviewer will still want to probe on this issue. Learn to differentiate between confidence and hubris, humility and self-effacement, and gratitude and entitlement.

Interviewers should be sensitive to the context within which most servicemembers and veterans experience the civilian job market. From the moment of enlistment, most of them are served doses of conflicting messages. Sometimes, they are told to expect to be embraced by a grateful nation that is eager to bestow high-paying jobs upon all veterans. At other times, they are told that veteran unemployment is chronic and utterly overwhelming for even the strongest of their peers. Of course, reality is somewhere in between, and the skilled interviewer will interpret conversations with servicemembers and veterans accordingly.

Ambition

Finally, the interviewer must determine the ambition of the candidate. Is this veteran who has retired after

20 years of service eager to build a second career at your company, or is he content to kick back and coast?

The good news is that most veterans aspire to continue to develop their leadership skills. They will often talk of "making a difference" and "getting a seat at the head table." Do not be concerned that candidates who say such things are too aggressive. Yes, cultural fit is critical, but remember that many veterans see all advancement as largely a function of exercises in leadership. They may not yet understand that salesmanship, operational efficiency, or administrative competence are equally and sometimes more valued in the civilian realm.

Be patient and compassionate. Wait for veterans to tell you how their ambition motivates them. Then consider carefully how well their ambition matches your company's need and culture.

Do not be intimidated by the prospect of interviewing veterans. Follow the three A's, and move three steps closer to identifying and attracting the high-quality veteran talent your team needs.

"I hired Scott specifically because I knew his leadership experience as a captain in the U.S. Army would enable him to shepherd this process to create a seamless product and to do so on time, and, just as importantly, without alienating the occasionally competing personalities from whom those details came. Indeed, military experience might be unique in equipping business leaders with this type of skill set."

Daniel Freifeld, CEO and Founder
Callaway Capital Management

Chapter 7
Challenges to Hiring Veterans

Of course, hiring veterans is not all puppies, unicorns, and rainbows. Certain specific challenges will vex even the savviest veteran hiring leader or line manager. Carried away by our enthusiasm to acquire high-quality veteran talent, we may neglect to address these challenges – to our peril.

Some of the challenges are "elephants in the room" that people would rather ignore than address. Better hiring and career outcomes result, however, when frank, honest dialogue uncovers underlying concerns.

Millennials and Males

Eighty-four percent of veterans are male, and most of them are demographically classified as "Millennial." A small industry of experts try to explain the quirks and general behavior tendencies of this cohort, and we will not replicate their research and speculations here. Suffice it to say that some of the values and behaviors attributed to veterans are really primarily those of all young men.

Personal Bias

Every imaginable category of diversity triggers some combination of stereotyping and generalization. Many of these are unfair, and some attitudes and/or attending actions may be correctly condemned as racist, sexist, homophobic, anti-Semitic, Islamophobic, or some other kind of unfair "-ist" or "-ic." An unfortunate reality of the politically correct times in which we live is that people are reluctant to admit and face their biases, whether they be negative or positive.

Despite widespread societal acceptance of the military as an institution worthy of respect and admiration, there are individuals who condemn military service and veterans on political, moral, or personal grounds. One may be a pacifist or simply a person who had a bad experience with a soldier or sailor. But regardless, it is important for recruiters and hiring managers to listen to their internal voices and directly confront veteran bias on a personal level.

Veteran bias can also be positive, so veteran hiring leaders must be aware of recruiters and hiring managers who tip the scales too far in favor of veterans. Many of us know a company leader who likes veterans so much that he or she might tend to overlook the warning signals from a veteran candidate.

As with other forms of diversity bias, truth, education, and patience are the very best antidotes. Many managers who may or may not admit to an anti-veteran prejudice will come around when exposed to enough high-quality candidates.

Cultural Apprehension

A related stereotype is that veterans are all former drill instructors or mindless, order-following automatons. Whether due to personal experience or a naïve absorption of Hollywood narratives, many corporate personnel bring to their evaluation of veteran talent a mindset that can be as ignorant as any sort of racial or gender bias.

The best way to "out" these biases is by encouraging people to articulate them. Sometimes, just hearing the articulation of their emotional preconceptions shows people that their fears are unfounded and even ignorant.

Post-Traumatic Stress

Advances in battlefield medicine, general awareness, and social media have intensified the spotlight of attention on Post Traumatic Stress (PTS) in recent years.[10] According to the Rand Corporation, fewer than 16% of combat veterans experience any sort of PTS.[11] In most cases, their reaction is simply jumpiness, bouts of sadness, sleep deprivation, or other non-violent symptoms.

10

Note the absence of the pejorative word "Disorder" from the acronym PTS. Increasingly, medical professionals are considering PTS as the normal reaction of a healthy brain to trauma rather than as a disorder or sickness.

11

http://www.veteransandptsd.com/PTSD-statistics.html

In fact, the vast majority of PTS sufferers are not violent, and they represent no greater threat than any other comparatively young person. Remember also that many veterans have never experienced combat.

And consider the fact that a large number of sexual assault victims in the United States experience PTS as a result of their ordeals.[12] Ask yourself what kind of organization would screen out applicants with such ordeals in their histories? It would be an unacceptable outrage.

Traumatic Brain Injury

We are also learning more about Traumatic Brain Injury (TBI) medically and sociologically. As in the case of PTS, however, there is a lot of misinformation about the prevalence and impact of TBI. Subject to regular employment laws about disability, TBI sufferers and other service-disabled veterans must be treated equitably if their value is to be realized.

---

[12]

http://www.ptsd.va.gov/public/types/violence/child-sexual-abuse.asp

Leadership Expectation

Many civilians who have no experience with the military fail to understand how intensely all branches of the service teach, celebrate, and enforce high ideals of leadership. This is not to say that all military leaders are skilled or effective. But it does mean that veterans of all levels can identify good leadership, or an absence thereof, in any organization.

The ideals of military leadership are diverse in theory and practice, and they vary according to the cultures of different units and services. But all contain elements of what the civilian world calls servant leadership. This means that all activity must support the mission and/ or contribute to team welfare. Leaders are expected to be selfless and utterly dedicated to the well-being of the individuals and team members they lead.

Thus, when veterans transition to the civilian world and encounter managers and leaders who are more selfish and short-sighted, they can become disillusioned. Or, phrased more positively, veterans make all managers "up their game" when it comes to matters of team and company leadership

Entitlement

When I consider the mixed messaging that attends veteran employment in the United States, I am not surprised that some veterans enter the civilian world with a strong sense of entitlement. Like any other group that has bene-fited from set-asides and priorities, they can become surly or impatient when such benefits are not forthcoming.

Usually, this feeling of entitlement is just temporary and will dissipate once the veteran encounters enough experience with the "real world." That said, it is per-missible, if not advisable, for civilian leadership to "pop the bubble" of any veteran who does not think he has to carry his own weight.

Regulatory Burden

Elsewhere in this handbook, I address the OFCCP, USERRA, tax credits, and other regulatory agencies and laws. For purposes of this chapter, it is enough to state the obvious – that veteran candidates bring along some "bag-gage" in the form of a need to comply in various ways.

Retention

Finally, there is mixed research regarding the reten-tion rates of veterans in their first post-service roles. Some say that veterans are more loyal than other work-ers; others point out the opposite. The intuitive fact remains, however, that transitioning veterans often do not know what to expect in the civilian world, so they may settle for a new job that is not a good fit for their skills and interests. Thus, veteran hiring leaders should track veteran-retention statistics and otherwise evalu-ate their experience with veteran employees.

"A people that values its privileges above its principles soon loses both."

President Dwight D. Eisenhower

Chapter 8
Special Categories

Service-Disabled Veterans

Many organizations like the idea of hiring disabled workers because of idealism, desire to tap into underserved labor pools, OFCCP compliance, or cynical optics. But some are surprised to learn that service-disabled veterans do not "look the way they are supposed to." Because of the prevalence of PTS, TBI, and other unseen wounds, many disabled veterans look conventionally normal.

Reservists and Guardsmen

Members of the reserve components of all services and both the Air and Army National Guard present challenges for employers. They need to follow the Uniformed Services Employment and Reemployment Rights Act of 1994 (USERRA), a federal law that establishes rights and responsibilities for uniformed servicemembers and their civilian employers.

Briefly, civilian employers have certain responsibilities and rights with regard to reservists and guardsmen, and must support their need to train and potentially deploy. When in doubt and company policy and common sense do not suffice, consult a lawyer who is conversant with USERRA.

Dishonorable Discharges

Although it seems counterintuitive, it is not prudent to ask a veteran whether he has been honorably discharged. According to Lisa Rosser of Value of a Veteran, "State and Federal Equal Employment Opportunity (EEO) laws do not prohibit you from asking about the type of discharge. However, asking a veteran to reveal the nature ('characterization of service' in military parlance) of their discharge is considered private information, similar to asking someone 'what kind of a disability do you have?'" [13]

Spouses

Military spouses, most of whom are wives, sacrifice in many ways almost as arduously as their military member. As a result, some employers make a laudable effort to reach out to that community as a talent pool. It is important to remember, however, that unlike veterans, spouses have not been vetted, do not count for regulatory purposes, and have not received the training of actual veterans.

That said, veteran spouses can offer skills and experience to organizations that are able to offer flexibility for their peripatetic lifestyles.

13

https://thevalueofaveteran.wordpress.com/2013/02/18/can-i-ask-a-veteran-about-the-type-of-military-discharge-he-received/

"The difficult we do immediately; the impossible takes a little longer."

Air Force motto

Chapter 9
What Do Veterans Want?

Savvy employers know that veterans often hold the solution to their continuing struggle to attract and retain high-quality talent. They understand that men and women who have military backgrounds possess skills, attitudes, and abilities beyond those of most people who have not served. Thus, veterans can add disproportionate value to any team or organization.

But as veteran unemployment drops to one of the lowest levels in years, hiring managers find themselves competing aggressively for this great talent pool. To compete effectively, companies need to ramp up their veteran-hiring strategies. They must develop outreach and branding tactics that communicate to veterans why their employment opportunities are worthy of consideration. At the core of this effort, companies must understand what most veterans seek as they transition to, or further develop, their civilian careers.

Veterans seek essentially the same features in their careers as everyone else, but two factors set veterans apart. One factor is the alacrity, focus, and dedication with which they seek these benefits. The other is that, due to their military experience, veterans tend to focus on certain special sets of needs. Successful hiring managers and recruiters should pay careful attention to these needs as they craft their veteran hiring and retention strategies.

One way to conceptualize and remember this universe of needs is an alliterative summary – The Four M's: Mission, Momentum, Money, and Mentorship. Companies that dependably and consistently deliver on the Four M's will find themselves assembling teams from the pool of America's finest talent – its veterans.

Mission

It should come as no surprise that a military-experienced candidate would find immense satisfaction in joining an organization whose mission resonates with his or her personal values and aspirations. While some join the military for college money, adventure, or specific experiences, virtually all enlist with an inspiration that stems from some level of idealism. So a team or a company that can make an authentic connection between its daily activities and a noble mission or higher purpose will attract and retain better veteran talent. The cause need not be dramatic or romantic. Not all companies can save an endangered species or cure a disease with their products or services. The takeaway: Companies that communicate with honesty and integrity in the execution of a worthy purpose will rise above others.

Millennial consumers of products, services, or employment opportunities – whether veterans or not

– also yearn for authenticity. Having grown up in a media-saturated world, these modern workers can spot a fake from miles away. They will, without compunction, avoid an organization that seems inauthentic.

Some veterans have experienced combat, and all have endured screening and training experiences that have matured them and sensitized them to the important things in life. The upside of this orientation is their dedication and determination when they buy into a cause. The downside? Any organization that just does not seem important will sustain no appeal for the applicant or employee.

Momentum

After 3 to 20 (or more) years in uniform, no veteran wants to step back in his or her next job. But too often, veterans fear that they will have to enter the civilian world a number of notches below their current stations. In some cases, this is just a matter of perception. But more often, it is a result of the rigidity of the employers' career-progression ladders.

Effective employers will examine their hiring practices to see that due credit is assigned for military experience, even when the nature of the work is not precisely that of the new role.

Job descriptions should be crafted carefully to be inclusive of military experience and education. For example, too often companies insist that a candidate possess a bachelor's degree when they really mean that they wish to attract someone who finishes stuff he or she starts and can write and communicate well. Many military experiences help generate these attributes. In the armed forces, people finish what they start because they have to. And good communication skills are essential when lives are at stake in urgent situations.

Money

All employees desire – and deserve – to be paid fairly for their contributions and labor. The challenge with veterans comes from their lack of understanding of their market value. Indeed, the very notion of market value can seem strange to transitioning veterans who come from a world of fixed "time-and-grade" pay scales that place importance on seniority and rank above demonstrated competence and reliability.

Education and transparency, therefore, are the keys to helping veterans make sense of civilian compensation arrangements. They need to understand the relationships among contribution, value, and pay and benefits. Employers that effectively lift the veil of secrecy regarding compensation paths and progressions will find that veterans will appreciate the direction and clarity in an area that might otherwise have baffled them.

Mentorship

While civilians speak of management and sometimes avoid the term "leadership," members of the military spend much of their time in the study and practice of the latter art. Most adhere to a simple but aspirational definition of leadership. Those so tasked will both accomplish their assigned mission and take care of their people. This dedication to the needs of team members can sometimes be lacking in a civilian environment strongly dedicated to profit or other arbitrary metrics. That environment can seem coldly devoid of human purpose or connection.

The expectations of military leadership are high. And while some commissioned and noncommissioned officers do not live up to these expectations on duty, many veterans expect some level of genuine leadership in their civilian jobs. Competitive employers will take leadership development seriously and dedicate resources to cultural development.

For years, corporate recruiters have been predicting a War for Talent. But because of the lingering effects of the Great Recession, that threat had receded. Now, employers are being called upon to sharpen their game if they wish to win. Because veterans are such a key component to an enlightened talent-acquisition strategy, any serious veteran-hiring effort will pay careful and consistent attention to the "Four M's" that the best veterans will seek and require.

"Honor to the soldier and sailor everywhere, who bravely bears his country's cause. Honor, also, to the citizen who cares for his brother in the field and serves, as he best can, the same cause."

Abraham Lincoln

Section III
How to Hire Veterans

Chapter 10
Understanding Motivations and Establishing Goals

All organizations fall somewhere on a spectrum that includes the following attitudes toward the hiring of veterans:

Hostile: Wants nothing to do with veterans.

Indifferent: Will hire veterans but accord them no preference or special treatment.

Open-minded: Will seek to understand the value of a veteran candidate, but only if doing so is not inconvenient.

Announced: Has proclaimed an intention to hire veterans, but has not yet dedicated resources or attention to making good on its proclamation. In recent years, it has become fashionable for companies to announce veteran-hiring programs and initiatives.

Committed: Has established measurable goals, internally understood objectives and rationales, and feedback mechanisms; has dedicated resources. This company "gets it," and is on the way to becoming exemplary.

Exemplary: Has reached the pinnacle of veteran-hiring excellence. Knows what it is looking for and where to find the talent. Has dedicated the necessary resources, measures the effectiveness of its initiative, fine-tunes its efforts, and makes its case to the veteran community clearly and effectively.

*"In the aftermath,
we are because they were."*

RJ Heller, *Holding Grace: Prose & Poetry*

Chapter 11
Branding

Hey, if I don't give y'all nothing else you better start at "What's your why?"
author and motivational speaker
Eric Thomas

Veterans are like any other employees in wanting to understand the why of your brand's offering. If you cannot succinctly articulate why someone should want to work for your company, how can you expect veterans to understand that?

Start with your unique selling proposition or your brand statement. This will be similar to what you communicate to all employees, but you need to be mindful of a few additional insights regarding veterans.

See Chapter 9 to better understand what most veterans seek in their civilian careers.

Authenticity is one concept that is critical in any branding effort. Veterans as a whole are expert at "sniffing out" insincerity and will know if your organization is faking or just going through the motions.

Do not be insulted if a veteran does not know much about your company at first. Yes, in this age of information ubiquity, it is difficult to forgive people who do not do their homework. On the other hand, if you spent the last year patrolling in Afghanistan or cruising under the Polar Icecap in a submarine, you might not have been able to keep up on the distinctions between Goodyear and Goodrich tires.

Key takeaways:
- Develop a brand statement for veterans.
- Be authentic.
- Be patient.
- Go where the veterans are, both physically and digitally.

"I've learned, Agent Sanders,
most warriors feel the same way
after they've come back from the battles
where men in expensive suits
and leather chairs send them.
We keep asking and asking you
to do the impossible and even when you succeed
it seems the world doesn't change all that much.
Don't let that diminish your sacrifice,
and that of your family waiting at home.
Your country is proud of you."

C.J. Hatch

Chapter 12
Engagement and Sourcing

This is not rocket science, but to hire veterans you need to encounter them. Or, in "infantry English," if you don't have veterans you can't have a veteran hiring program.[14]

There are a number of tactics for sourcing veteran talent. I will examine each in turn.

Career Fairs

Many recruiters swear by the benefits of attending career fairs. "Out of more than 30 live interviews from the event, the hiring rate was about 50% from one career fair that lasted four hours – a pretty good cost-per-hire," noted the director of human resources for a large state government agency.

One company that has subsidiaries across the country puts veteran job fairs at the top of its list for finding quality candidates. "We can solve a lot of hiring issues

---

14

Infantry English is a comical term used in the Army and less frequently in the Marine Corps to mean "phrased simply and clearly." It is meant to convey a certain sense of mockery of the intellectual resources of a typical infantryman but also contains an element of respect for the single-minded clarity of an American warrior. It is similar to the use of the word "laconic."

in one event," said the director of recruiting. "I frequently tell hiring managers at our subsidiaries: 'If you attend, you will find all the people you need.'"

An international logistics company attends career fairs exclusively to fill its talent pipeline, hiring more than 70 veterans in one year. The fairs are appealing because the company can choose to attend events taking place in the cities where it has the greatest needs. A national transportation company has hired more than 50 veterans exclusively from career fairs.

Another recruiting leader noted, "We've found that the military offers the discipline and training that produces motivated, successful employees. Job fairs are a great way to connect qualified veterans with our talent needs."

Many career fairs feature private areas for on-the-spot interviews. The ability to meet, assess, and speak in depth with candidates on-the-spot makes career fairs a cost-effective screening tool – saving time, coordination efforts, and resources.

Career fairs also work well for veterans. Many veteran candidates have reported that they interviewed with several companies at a single event, and were encouraged about the prospect of getting a job as a result. Others have reported that they left events with job offers in hand, along with multiple requests for interviews. Still others were contacted by several companies to interview within just a few days of the events they attended.

One veteran reported, "Overall, it was very successful for me because I got immediate feedback. I was interviewed at the site and shortly afterwards I was offered a job as an equipment operator. I'm very grateful."

Another said, "When I attended a career fair and was able to present myself in person, I had much greater success." She was able to tell recruiters about her work ethic and to describe her experience working in a variety of capacities.

As a side benefit, the publicity that arises in connection with a veteran career fair can be a boon. Often, radio and television reports will highlight the fact that local companies are giving local jobs to local veterans. These organizations then carry the distinction in their communities of being veteran-friendly.

Virtual Career Fairs (VCF's)

Since the dawn of the commercial Internet, providers have experimented with VCF's. Usually, after one strips away the hype, a VCF is really a multilateral chat box paired with some multimedia broadcasting.

Virtual career fairs can be efficient for very specific hiring needs across vast distances. For example, a medical clinic looking for an immunologist to move to Patagonia might benefit from assembling candidates from all over the world and conducting a VCF.

But for most conventional needs candidates find VCF's to be cold and clumsy. A company risks branding itself as remote and distant if it uses this tool too much.

Job Postings

Companies use job postings for a number of reasons:

- **Compliance** – to establish a record of veteran hiring efforts for regulatory purposes. If this is your goal, make sure you use a job board that has compliance technology embedded so that you can obtain the records if you are audited by the OFCCP.

- **Sourcing** – For specific positions (e.g., emergency room RN), postings can be an efficient way to source candidates. That efficiency drops off for more general positions (e.g., marketing manager).

Postings are most effective when they are broadly distributed and combined with a career fair, networking, and referral and email campaign programs.

Targeted Email Campaigns

A few veteran-hiring companies with databases will send targeted email campaigns to veterans in a certain geography or with certain skill sets. For example, an employer might send one or more emails to veterans with radar technology training within, say, fifty miles of a given airport or city. The art and science of making this tool work is having a description that is broad enough to be inclusive but specific enough to be targeted.

Candidate Databases

Many companies offer subscriptions, or search licenses, to their databases of job candidates who have military backgrounds. These "job boards" have grown and improved enormously in recent years. They can contain hundreds of thousands of registered veterans.

Job boards offer a number of ways to locate the right veteran for the job. They enable subscribers to:
- narrow searches progressively via search facets
- set up candidate search agents to get daily emails with fresh candidates
- share jobs with candidates
- forward candidate profiles to others in the searcher's organization
- use keywords to narrow searches
- save resumes to folders
- restrict searches by ZIP Code and geographic location

Sophisticated filtering techniques enable employers to conduct precise searches to targeted segments, and to deliver email messages at their convenience. These tools make database subscriptions an extremely cost-effective option for recruiters. As one employer said, "The search engine allowed us to select several specific criteria and find the right personnel very quickly."

Transitioning and veteran personnel often have strong inducements to register on these job boards, including access to hundreds of thousands of posted jobs, profile builders, integration with other social media sites, resume upload, and other job search-related resources.

Whatever a company's cost per hire, using cost-effective hiring practices to attract and retain the most talented people available is the best way to "work smart." Given veterans' strong training and leadership, in addition to their other intangible skills, a veteran hired is invariably a sound choice for any company's bottom line.

Third Party Recruiters

In the veteran hiring space, there has long been demand for contingency recruiters. Usually charging about 20% of first year's compensation, these recruiters specialize in placing junior officers (JMO's) and highly specialized senior enlisted personnel into hiring companies.

The benefits of using veteran contingency search firms are:
- pay only on placement
- outsourced effort
- generally quick – one to three months

The limitations are:

- expense
- pressure on candidates to accept positions that might not be good fits, resulting in high turnover during first year of employment
- lack of leverage or economies of scale – for example, four hires might cost $100,000; a focused media strategy with that sort of budget might generate 500 or more veteran hires

On-Base Access

Some companies like to recruit on or near military bases. The challenges here are:

- Most veterans do not intend to live near the base where they served.
- Access to bases can be challenging in a post-9/11 world.
- As a short-term solution, veterans may take jobs in places where they do not want to live.

Veteran Service Organizations (VSO's)

There are tens of thousands of VSO's in the United States. Most fall under one or more of the following categories:

Community Service. Organizations such as the American Legion sponsor youth sports, parades, speech contests, and citizenship prizes.

Fraternal. Some VSO's exist largely for the social benefit of their members. A Veterans of Foreign Wars post might be a gathering spot for older veterans. Team Red, White & Blue might organize teams of runners or cyclists among younger veterans.

Continued Service. Organizations like Team Rubicon and The Mission Continues give veterans a chance to do what they do best – continue to serve.

Advocacy. Groups such as DAV (Disabled American Veterans) exist mainly to provide support and services to veterans according to their needs

Political Influence. Many VSO's have their headquarters in Washington, D.C. They locate there because they seek to influence federal policy, especially regarding benefits and services.

Commemoration. Many national and local organizations are focused on historical commemoration and preservation. Their projects include oral history as well as the construction and maintenance of memorials.

Education and Member Service. VSO's like the U.S. Naval Institute serve as think tanks and non-profit publishers.

Government Efforts

One issue upon which our fractured political classes can agree is service to veterans. Those on the right typically like the military and the its missions. Those on the left may not fully support all of the military's goals, but care about the well-being of veterans during and after their service ends.

Unfortunately, most government efforts for veterans fail because they usually start with the veteran-as-victim mindset, and they are hopelessly bureaucratic and inefficient. There are some good resources at the city, county, and state levels in some areas. But for the most part, free government resources offer what you pay for them, nothing.

*"As anyone who has experienced it will know,
war is many contradictory things.
There is brutality and heroism, comedy and tragedy,
friendship, hate, love and boredom.
War is absurd yet fundamental,
despicable yet beguiling,
unfair yet with its own strange logic.
Rarely are people 'back home' exposed
to these contradictions — society tends only
to highlight those qualities it needs,
to construct its own particular narrative."*

Tim Hetherington, *Infidel*

Chapter 13
Understanding and Using Cost per Hire

Cost per hire (CPH) measures the cost-effectiveness of an organization's recruiting operation. Ideally, cost effectiveness means hiring the most talented people in the shortest amount of time for the least expense.

Employers can use CPH:
- as a benchmark to compare departments
- for budget planning
- to measure recruiting performance and process efficiency
- as a factor in strategic planning
- to determine whether, or by how much, to outsource its recruiting process

Because organizations use various methods to calculate their hiring costs, it is difficult to arrive at a figure that represents an average CPH. According to one source, the average CPH for all U.S. companies stands at about $3,479, with organizations of 10,000 or more employees coming in at $1,949.[15] The average cost of recruiting a new college graduate during the 2011-2012 recruiting season was $5,134, according to the National Association of Colleges and Employers' (NACE) *2012 Recruiting Benchmarks Survey*.[16] NACE estimates that the cost for making an entry-level hire over the past few years has ranged from $5,700 to $8,900 – including college recruiting salaries, expense reimbursement, travel, relocation, etc.

Although employers from coast to coast have launched their own veteran hiring initiatives, navigating the veteran space can be confusing at times. One employer remarked, "It can be overwhelming and confusing for employers who are just trying to start hiring veterans because they don't know which resource is reputable, or where to start." [17]

Using a full-service veteran hiring authority with access to a large veteran population is one way to source quality veteran candidates. These firms build, refresh, and maintain veteran candidate pipelines and serve as rallying points for creating long-term veteran hiring initiatives. Career fairs and databases are two avenues for employers to recruit "in bulk," and to get the biggest bang for their hiring buck. Military-to-civilian hiring firms such as RecruitMilitary offer both of these options, among other recruiting tools.

15

Bersin & Associates, 2011. NACE's 2012 Recruiting Benchmarks Survey.

16

NACE's 2012 Recruiting Benchmarks Survey.

17

Margaret C. Harrell and Nancy Berglass, "Employing America's Veterans: Perspectives from Business" (Center for a New American Security, June 2012).

Veteran Hiring Tax Credits

It is important to note that veteran-recruitment CPH comes with tax credits through the Work Opportunity Tax Credit (WOTC) program. This is a federal tax credit available to employers for hiring individuals from certain target groups, one of these being veterans. The current Act extends the WOTC program through December 31, 2019.

Tax credits available for hiring qualifying veterans range from $2,400 to $9,600 per veteran hired. Eligible veterans are those who have a service-connected disability, are unemployed, or are receiving SNAP (food stamp) benefits. Veterans qualify by being unemployed for as little as 4 weeks. Employees must work at least 120 hours in the first year of employment to receive the tax credit.

Though this is a federal tax credit program, there are differences within each state, so be sure to either contact your State Workforce Agency, or utilize a company that is established to help other companies navigate the process to receive these credits. Recruit-Military is partnered with leading companies providing this service. One very important point to remember regardless of the state you are in is that IRS Form 8850 and ETA Form 9061 must be submitted within 28 calendar days of the employee's start date.

To learn more about eligibility requirements for

these potentially valuable tax credits, visit the WOTC website, http://www.doleta.gov/wotc, and for more information on how to claim the tax credit, visit the IRS website, http://www.irs.gov.

Interviewing and Screening Veterans

When most corporate recruiters and hiring managers interview a veteran, they treat the process as if the veteran were just like any other candidate. On one level, this is good, because it ensures equality of opportunity and compliance with both human resources law and common sense.

Companies lose out on the high value of veteran talent, however, when they do not take certain specific steps to prepare, assess, and follow up with veteran candidates. And one model for successful veteran interviewing is defined by the acronym PAF: Prepare, Assess, and Follow up. The preparation phase is key, so I will cover it in detail in the remainder of this chapter.

Why are you hiring veterans?

During the preparation phase, the interviewer reviews the organization's driving purpose for hiring veterans, checks his or her bias regarding veterans, and seeks to understand the true success drivers for the open position.

Most interviewers skip the first step, but it is critical to understand what motivates the organization's veteran hiring initiative. Does the company have a sincere commitment to bring the abilities and experiences of veterans on board, or is it more about branding and the company's image?

Organizations can often feature a wide range of sometimes conflicting motivations. The skilled interviewer will seek to understand the "why" – and not just the "what" – of the hiring initiative. Only by understanding the organization's purpose will the interviewer be able to interpret levels of tolerance for training and acculturation.

Check your bias

Related to this issue, the interviewer must check his or her bias regarding veterans as employees. In our politically correct times, any admission of preconceived notions about any group of people is interpreted as the worst possible sin. Yet it is impossible to exist in our media-saturated culture without developing some predetermined notions about any group – whether accurate or not. Rather than suppress these thoughts, the interviewer should get in touch with them and confront them with facts.

For example, it would be perfectly normal to feel that all former soldiers are control-freak fascists because your sister-in-law was briefly married to one. But experience and reason will teach you that such generalizations are both inaccurate and unfair. Only by listening to your inner voice and challenging it will you overcome your bias – which can be positive as well as negative – and learn to make better and more informed decisions.

Research military experience

The interviewer need not understand every line in a military resume. However, a veteran candidate will certainly appreciate a basic understanding of general military terms and experiences. Some civilian interviewers do not understand the difference between a submarine and a U.S. Marine.

Your organization can designate one or more veteran employees to serve as sounding boards. Most veterans can explain the general background of another veteran's resume, or at least help the interviewer prepare a few good clarifying questions.

Open-ended questions followed by polite clarifying comments can help structure the portion of the interview regarding military experience. For example: "Please walk me through your military experience from your enlistment through your initial training and your ultimate assignment to a field unit. I am eager to understand why you did the things you did and what you learned from each experience." If the candidate uses jargon you do not follow, it is perfectly all right to ask for a clarification. For example: "I am sorry, I am not sure I understand what a boatswain's mate does. Can you explain?"

Understand the real job requirements

Finally, the interviewer must seek to have a deep, intuitive, and clear understanding of the real job requirements. Most organizations publish multiple-page job descriptions that contain requirements for certifications and skills having little to do with the task at hand. Experienced hiring managers and recruiters compensate for this verbosity with a short-hand understanding of the true needed skills and attributes.

For example: "The customer-service manager really needs to be good with people and motivating his team on a daily basis, even while being regularly berated by obnoxious customers." When properly understood this way, it quickly becomes clear how an infantry squad leader who led patrols day after day in hostile territory while maintaining personal and team morale would likely excel in the job.

Armed with the preparation steps detailed above, an interviewer is ready to conduct the meeting and assess the qualifications of the veteran applicant in a way that is effective, accurate, and most likely to result in the desired outcomes.

"Nearby sat a veteran in a wheelchair.
He was young, handsome, and athletic,
through missing a leg.

My daughter went to him and asked,
"You're army - right?"

He said, "Yes, I am."

My daughter hugged him.
"Thank you," she said.
Tears welled in the man's eyes.

"Did you get my card?" she asked.
"My school sent you a card.
It said, 'Thank you for saving our Earth.'"

The guy just about lost it.
He said, "You're welcome. Yes, we did get your card.
Thank you for doing that."

- Michael Sobel, son of Herbert Sobel.
Michael talking about his 6-year-old daughter
meeting veterans.

Marcus Brotherton,
We Who Are Alive and Remain:
Untold Stories from the Band of Brothers

Chapter 14
The Roles of Corporate Leaders
in Veteran Hiring

In most American corporations, managers at various levels and in different functions have unique roles to play.

Chief executive officer (CEO)

The CEO sets the strategic direction and sees that resources are allocated to ensure the accomplishment of the mission. When it comes to veteran hiring, a clear top-down vision statement can help create a climate of focus for veteran hiring. This mandate, if well executed, can create effective "air cover" for subordinate leaders who take chances in hiring veterans.

Vice president of human resources

The HR vice president executes the talent strategy across the organization. Elements of the strategy include compliance, talent acquisition, diversity and inclusion, benefits administration, and sometimes training. It is at this level that an HR leader can set priories and allocate resources to ensure effective outcomes in veteran hiring.

Talent acquisition manager

At the level of talent acquisition manager, the rubber meets the road on execution. The manager must have a branding strategy and an engagement plan in place to effectively realize the promise of a good veteran hiring initiative.

Talent acquisition leaders commonly see veteran hiring as yet another mandate from higher-ups who do not really understand the day-to-day strain of their efforts. Keeping veteran hiring a priority, not just an object of lip service, usually falls to in-house recruiters and hiring managers.

Diversity & inclusion (D&I) manager

D&I is a broad and growing function at many companies. D&I managers often feel pulled in too many directions because they are usually given a myriad of diversity goals, which can include gender, race, sexual orientation, and veteran status. And because they are stretched thin, the managers can also feel insufficiently trained and insufficiently aware of the diversity benefits of some classes. But the regulatory teeth of the OFCCP and other government agencies give the D&I team leverage beyond simple morality and business logic to get the attention of C-suite executives.

Line managers/hiring managers

This broad category includes all of the future bosses of our veterans. Usually, these leaders are more concerned with talent quality than they are with abstract compliance or D&I goals. Often, they need to be won over to the merits of hiring veterans. The good news is that, once onboard, they typically become the strongest advocates of veteran hiring.

Typical Scenarios

Does any of these scenarios sound familiar?

- The CEO has just returned from a trip to Washington, D.C., where she had a photo op at the White House. She now wants to "do more to hire veterans . . ." She turns to the VP of HR and says, "Bob, I want to hire more veterans. What is your plan?"

- The VP of human resources is primarily focused on launching compliance training programs, slowing the rate of employee turnover in the retail division, and complying with aggressive affirmative action programs. Now the CEO says that the company needs to start hiring more veterans, yesterday. What does he do now?

- Talent Acquisition is already having a hard time locating employees with the technical and interpersonal skills needed to thrive in the company's rapidly changing industry. Now, the VP of HR says they have to "do more" to hire veterans. Is this one more hassle or an opportunity to "kill two birds with one stone?"

- The D&I director worked at a Historically Black College for ten years before coming to XYZ Inc. to head its diversity program. In the early years, this was largely understood to mean African-American outreach and hiring. Even though the director's great-grandfather was a Harlem Hellfighter who won a Croix de Guerre in the trenches of France during World War I, she knows very little about the military. Now she is being asked to start a veteran hiring initiative.

- A unit manager is responsible for sales and operations throughout the Southwest Region. Despite his best efforts, 25% of his positions are unfilled, and he is spending one day per week just interviewing. He has just been told that veteran hiring has become a corporate priority. How can he get comfortable with the idea that veterans may be a partial answer to his needs and not another distraction?

"Damn the wars but bless the soldier."

T.L. Moffitt

Chapter 15
Measuring and Celebrating Success

Most veteran hiring programs focus primarily on recruitment, with less effort placed on managing or retaining veteran employees once they are hired. Although employers perceive that their veteran employees perform well, many do not collect metrics about veteran performance and retention. There are a number of metrics that organizations may consider when evaluating their veteran hiring initiatives, including:

- The number of veterans hired
- The percentage of all hires that are veterans
- Outside recognition of the company or veteran employment program (e.g., awards or publicity)
- The number of veterans that reached later-round interviews
- The range of business levels to which veterans are hired
- The extent to which hiring has led the company to be branded as veteran-friendly

Although these metrics are useful, they are not sufficient to truly evaluate the merit and effectiveness of veteran recruitment efforts. Other measures are needed to properly justify the level of effort and investment the company has dedicated to veteran employment, and assess outcomes beyond recruitment as well as the long-term impact on the company.

Every employer's goal is to hire the best talent, but how can that be measured? The two key metrics that matter most when evaluating the success of any recruitment program are performance and retention.

While decreasing cost per hire is desirable, increasing the quality of hire is a game-changer. The reason is simple – great employees deliver better performance, more revenue, and higher profits. That holds true for any new hire, not just veterans. Many employers do not collect or analyze veterans' performance data, mostly because it is difficult to correlate performance data with veteran employees and there are no established performance metrics in place. However, if such metrics were put in place, they could provide a compelling argument to continue investing in veteran hiring programs. Since there is no standard formula for determining quality, one way to measure would be for recruiters and hiring managers to define the criteria for quality before recruiting. Quality of hire can then be measured through a simple survey that lists each criterion and asks the hiring manager how the employee meets each standard.

"To The Veterans of the United States of America

Thank you, for the cost you paid
for our freedom, thank you for the freedom
to live in safety and pursue happiness,
for freedom of speech (thus my book),
and for all the freedoms
that we daily take for granted."

Sara Niles, *Torn From the Inside Out*

Chapter 16
Other Duties of Veteran Hiring Leaders

Executives charged with hiring and retaining veterans are often responsible for other veteran-related duties. For example:

- Veteran-related company events and ceremonies like Veteran's Day or Memorial Day celebrations. A tip here is to tap into your company's Veteran Employee Resource Group or club for help. Local veteran service organizations, reserve units, and even ROTC units at nearby colleges can help.
- Veteran-related charity events like the United Way drive.
- Creation and operation of Employee Resource Groups (ERG's). ERG's can be great tools for planning and executing strategies for attracting and retaining veteran talent. The keys to making an ERG work are:
  - Empowering them with a real purpose
  - Placing a motivated veteran in charge
  - Supporting them with resources
  - Telling their story throughout the company

"This nation will remain the land of the free only so long as it is the home of the brave."

Elmer Davis

Chapter 17
Veteran Retention

To understand the true extent of the costs involved in hiring a new employee, it's important to look at retention rates. Hiring costs don't come just from direct expenses associated with hiring a new employee; they also include the costs associated with finding and training a replacement if the employee resigns. The cost of losing an employee can be as high as 3-4 times their annual salary.

Retention metrics are easier to implement and track than performance metrics, but many employers face challenges in collecting this data specifically for veteran employees. However, tracking to see if veterans stay longer than other employees with similar characteristics – education level, years of experience, salary level – could help to justify the resources spent on veteran hiring initiatives.

Suggested ways to collect this data include looking at the turnover rate for a specific role and comparing that to the turnover rate across specific departments. Employers can also try checking the turnover rate by pay grade – for example, looking at how many resignations vs. terminations there have been by department, role, or pay grade. A proper analysis of this metric is best performed every 3-6 months and graded across a period of time to show trends.

*"Some people live an entire lifetime
and wonder if they have ever
made a difference in the world,
but the Marines don't have that problem."*

Ronald Reagan

Section IV
The Veteran's Perspective

Chapter 18
Common Misconceptions of Veteran Job Seekers

As a veteran hiring leader, you may find yourself in a position to counsel veterans whom you cannot, or will not, hire for your own organization. Doing this kind of work makes for good karma and can build your personal professional brand and that of your company.

One challenge you will have is that veterans are fed a lot of bad information during their transition classes and from society as a whole. In this chapter, I will address some of the larger misconceptions.

Much of the following is adapted from my series of online articles titled "Lies They Tell Transitioning Veterans." I intended these articles for a veteran audience. I hope they help you as a veteran counselor.

For some years, all transitioning military personnel have been required to complete career planning classes before they leave active service. Known by acronyms like TAP (Transition Assistance Program), ACAP (Army Career Alumni Program), or GPS (Goals, Plans, Success), these classes aim to confer to the soon-to-be veteran the skills, attitudes, and contacts he or she will need to conduct an effective job search. During those precious hours, well-intentioned contract instructors labor to convey the best-practices experiences of the thousands of personnel who have transitioned before.

Much of the content is good, like how to write a resume, but many of the learning points are unhelpful at best and damaging at worst. The teachers struggle to hold the attention of men and women who are daydreaming of home, and the servicemembers learn many lessons that will be damaging to their transitions. Veteran job seekers who are ambitious and strongly driven to succeed will do well to beware of these counterproductive messages and, in many cases, do the opposite of what is taught.

MOS is not destiny

First, we look at the message that one's assigned Military Occupational Specialty ("MOS") will dictate one's civilian career options.

In the past few years, "experts" have tried to explain much of the disconnect between the demand for effective workers and the supply of high-quality veteran talent by saying that those who have the demand simply do not understand those who constitute the supply.

According to this view, if the hiring company or the veteran job seeker were simply to insert his or her MOS code into a software box, an algorithm could translate the military job experience into a civilian job title that would make sense. But most MOS translation software is either humorously obvious (e.g., an Army truck driver can drive civilian trucks) or discouragingly limited (an infantry sergeant should be a security guard). For most veterans, these software programs are an exercise in limiting their options rather than expanding them.

Veterans spend an inordinate amount of time focused on the superficial terminology of their resumes, and become restricted in what they think they are qualified to do. Instead, job seekers should think of their MOS's like college majors. Thus, if an MOS is directly applicable to a civilian job that the veteran wants to continue (e.g., medical technician, pilot, or electrician), he should use it to demonstrate his fit and qualification. If not, as with those who served in combat arms, he should use it to demonstrate intangible characteristics rather than specific job skills.

For example, a former Army Ranger should have no trouble communicating that he would be tough, team-oriented, and doggedly determined to accomplish his quota in a sales job.

Who you are is much more important than what you were classified to do in the military. If the direct aspects of your experiences in the military are not compelling in the civilian job market, think about how those experiences might be valuable in the civilian market on a conceptual level. For example, there is little demand for computing artillery firing data in the civilian world but there is tremendous need for people who can work with numbers on teams with very tight deadlines and lots of pressure. Concentrate on communicating those benefits rather than apologizing that you do not fit exactly the enumerated job skills of the civilian position.

Military experience is in high demand in the civilian world, so veteran unemployment is lower than civilian employment. Veterans make great employees. Have confidence in who you are and what you are capable of accomplishing. Tell your story. Do not let any piece of software or a misguided classification of your experience hold you back.

Passive networking is not effective

Most transition classes provide at least a passing mention of the power of networking and the importance of setting up a LinkedIn profile. But few of these classes communicate the fact that networking is hard and active work. There is no such thing as effective easy and passive networking. The idea that one can just set up a LinkedIn profile and wait for jobs to appear is a common misconception.

LinkedIn is like an old-fashioned phone book. You need to be properly listed, but the listing itself is no substitute for face-to-face interaction and a clear job search plan. Yes, the job seeker should give careful attention to her online brand via LinkedIn and other social media. But at the same time, she must understand that profiles and pages alone are not networking.

As the CEO of RecruitMilitary, I get thousands of LinkedIn invitations from transitioning veterans every year. Of all these potential contacts, only a handful send reasonable, focused, and actionable networking requests. The others apparently think that reaching out and connecting is the end goal in itself.

A job seeker must first be able to articulate exactly what he seeks. Then he must engage with real people to obtain the information, personal referrals, and candid feedback needed to move closer to his objective. He must do this in a spirit of mutual interest relative to the other party. Each face-to-face meeting or telephone conversation must convey:

- who I am – the introduction
- what I am trying to accomplish – the goal
- how you can help (typically with information, referrals, and/or feedback) – the ask
- how I can help you? – the give

Through a vigorous and iterative sequence of meetings, phone calls, and encounters, the veteran job seeker will cultivate an ever-expanding network of human contacts who can provide the information and connections that he needs.

Paradoxically, effective networking is both aggressive and indirect. One does not ask for jobs directly, but seeks to learn more about career options and to help the people met along the networking road. The conversations with those you meet are called information interviews. If you meet with someone who is able to hire you, she will let you know if she has a job opening. If, like most contacts, she does not have an immediate job opening, she will refer you to others and/or teach you something.

The critical takeaway is that the job seeker must help others help him. Most people want to help job seekers in general and veterans in particular, but they cannot read minds and they will not do your work for you.

Each networking meeting enables you to display your character, curiosity, maturity, and focus. You will learn to "get your rap down." As you continue these meetings, and if you do your homework and listen closely, you will become more knowledgeable and insightful, and therefore more impressive. You will exude the confidence that comes from knowing who you are and what you are trying to accomplish – and from beginning to see how you are going to get there.

"I don't know, maybe I'd like to work with numbers or something" becomes "I learned in the Navy Supply Corps that details and process are prerequisites for overall success. I am focused on finding a midlevel analytical role in a manufacturing or services company where I can apply my mathematics and logic ability on problems of cost accounting or operating efficiency problems."

There is no way that you can learn to position yourself professionally without meeting and engaging with people, learning how the world works, and trying on roles for size. This is the essence of networking. Like patrolling in the infantry, it is active, engaging and, if done right, more than a little unnerving.

Make no mistake; networking is hard and active work. You should break a sweat and be exhausted at the end of every day of your job search. If you are not, frankly you are not working hard enough. Remember, you did not get through boot camp by hitting send buttons on online applications and expecting the world to find you.

Career fairs work

As CEO of the nation's leading producer of veteran career fairs, I have heard from some candidates that their transition instructors discouraged them from attending such events. This is classic bad advice.

As a Marine, I remember being on liberty in some exotic port city and walking by a club. A shipmate who was leaving the place – and who was obnoxiously tipsy at the moment – declared loudly that the club was a waste of time and money. My friends and I might well have disregarded that advice, entered the club, and ended up having a great evening discussing the great books and contemporary literature with the locals.

It is the same with high-quality veteran career fairs. There is always some know-it-all who is prepared to dismiss the activity even as others are wildly successful.

Our own RecruitMilitary numbers prove this, with 80% of job seeker attendees recommending the expos they attended, while the remaining 20% do not recommend those same events.

Well-run veteran career fairs are a great way to establish contacts and relationships, obtain information about opportunities, and directly apply for jobs. You probably will not achieve all of these objectives at each table, but if you work a fair with the right plan and the right attitude, the event will serve as a critical component of an effective job search.

Here are some misconceptions that prevent veterans from making the most of career fairs:

The employers are not serious about hiring. Just because an organization does not seem interested in you does not mean that it is not serious about veteran hiring. Companies pay $1,295 to attend our career fairs, and they have to pay the salaries of two or more employees for the day. Why would an organization do this if it did not want to hire veterans? To "wave the flag?" There are much cheaper and more ostentatious ways to show support for the troops than attending career fairs.

Recruiters attend veteran career fairs because they suspect or know that veterans are the answer to one or more of their talent needs. All organizations need great people. Veterans are great people. Therefore, all organizations need veterans.

Not all employers will take my resume, so why should I attend? Unfortunately, some companies interpret federal law to mean that they cannot accept resumes at a career fair. This has to do with OFCCP rules that are, ironically, designed to help veterans and other groups with companies that work federal contracts. I will spare the political commentary, but the rules are not the fault of the employers. For a job seeker, the way to handle this problem is to apply online before the fair and bring a copy of the online confirmation form from the company's applicant tracking system. This will help the career fair exhibitor give you candid feedback and track your application.

The companies do not have jobs that would interest me. Veterans commonly make the mistake of assuming that certain companies do not have the types of jobs that they seek. Knowing this, we encourage job seekers to talk to all of the employers. How would the candidates know that, for example, a grocery chain hires a lot more than cashiers or that a bank is looking for many functions beyond tellers?

A job seeker should research the company attendees ahead of time, know what sorts of positions they seek to fill, and come prepared with an action plan for the fair. They should not presume to know what a company needs just by its signage or brand name.

All veteran career fairs are the same. Some veteran career fairs are produced by organizations that have a surfeit of good intentions but lack access to employers or the logistical skills to operate successful events. Sometimes veterans conclude that, just because one event they attended was substandard, the entire category lacks purpose. Think about it, would you foreswear all restaurants because of one poor meal?

Attend veteran career fairs produced by reputable companies. Judge the events by the quality of the organizations represented. And appreciate that your success at the fairs is primarily up to you.

There are too many schools at the career fair. Veterans are sometimes irked by the number of schools and universities that attend career fairs. Quite reasonably, the job seekers want a paycheck and not a tuition bill.

But most schools are skilled marketers. They attend these fairs because they know that the events work. If they enroll one student as a result of a fair, they are generally happy. In addition, some schools are actually hiring personnel at the fairs. So, if you are not interested in furthering your education and you are sure you do not want to work at a school, just bypass the school's table and go to the next one.

Working a career fair is a microcosm of the whole job-search experience. You need to project a positive mental attitude, know what you seek to accomplish, and have a plan for achieving your goal. Whether it is gathering information, making networking contacts, or obtaining actual job interviews, if you know what constitutes success, you are more likely to achieve it.

All that said, working a high-quality veterans career fair should not be the only part of your job search. Do not listen to naysayers who dismiss any smart and productive job-search tactic. Usually they are the ones who miss out, while you take another positive step in your career.

Job search is not harder for veterans

We have all heard that veterans have a harder time than any other group of people when it comes to getting jobs. According to this narrative, civilians cannot understand MOS designations or rank structures, and the military-civilian cultural divide is too wide. Buying into the narrative, some veterans defeat themselves in their job search before they even get started. But is the narrative accurate? Are we psyching ourselves out before the game even begins?

Question: What do veterans, women, law school graduates, Latinos, college graduates, young people, middle-aged people, older people, European-Americans, members of the LGBT community, and African-Americans have in common?

Answer: All have been subjects of recent media or research coverage citing that they are experiencing an unemployment crisis.

How can it be that virtually all Americans, including educated white men, can readily classify themselves as part of a group that finds job search especially challenging? If there is no segment of American society that has not been the subject of a journalistic piece decrying how it has a harder time when it comes to getting jobs, how useful is the distinction? The cold, hard truth is that job search and career transition are challenging for everyone.

It is human nature to blame circumstances out of our control for our condition. And the incessant drumbeat of superficial media desperate to fill a 24-hour news cycle will default to "veterans-as-victims" clichés. This may have resonated in the 1970's, when an alienated, unpopular, and drafted military returned to civilian life. But that was two generations ago, an eternity in today's fast-paced economy.

The successful veteran job seeker will resist blaming group identity for poor job-search results. A positive attitude is the foundation of any efficacious job search, and blaming others for one's fate reeks of negativity. Like most achievements in life, career success is a function of hard work, talent, focus, self-knowledge, market knowledge, and luck. Group identity is low on the list of factors that matter.

Yet bias in the marketplace is real. Veterans will encounter both recruiters and hiring managers who are hostile or indifferent to veterans on political, moral, or cultural grounds. And there is widespread ignorance regarding the nature and prevalence of conditions like Post Traumatic Stress and Traumatic Brain Injury.

Most of these attitudinal barriers can be overcome by means of patient, persuasive interpersonal communication and education. Where one encounters the small minority who simply refuse to consider a veteran candidate, it is better to move on to other opportunities. Any organization or individual who is so ill-informed as to not recognize the value of a veteran's experience and talent is not worthy to benefit from his or her future service anyway.

Furthermore, bias can be profoundly positive as well as negative. When one thinks back to 2008, it was easy for the media to find some bigot to say that he would not consider voting for Barrack Obama because of his race. And yet, many voters of all persuasions chose his candidacy primarily because of his race. In other words, what was a negative for some was a compellingly positive characteristic for others.

So it is with veteran status. The aggressive veteran job seeker will likely find many more employers positively inclined toward veterans than against.

Psychologists speak of the concept of agency. It is the belief that people can affect their own environments and destinies. Those with a strong sense of agency experience the job-search process as a series of challenges that can be overcome through hard work and talent.

People without agency stand by as the world happens to them, rather than the other way around.

The good news is that veterans are indeed in high demand. Veteran unemployment is at record lows. Because of their service and quality, veterans have access to an expansive network of civilians who are only too pleased to offer information, advice, and access to those who ask for it.

When you hear the inner voice of doubt dragging down your job search, return to basics. Do you know what you are good at? Do you know what you want to do? Do you know the right people to provide the information and access to others to be successful? In most cases, ineffective job seekers have not done the work necessary to be successful in their career searches. It is never productive to dwell on the negative messages associated with group identity. If you are a United States military veteran, you are better than that. Keep working hard and smart. You are closer than you may realize to the career you seek.

You are a hero; you are a loser

During the mid-1980's, when I was a young battalion intelligence officer in the Marine Corps, we used to joke that every threat briefing would depict the Soviets and their allies as either undefeatable supermen or pathetic losers. One day, they would show pictures of Swedish actor Dolph Lundgren as a Spetsnaz super-warrior and emphasize the 5:1 ratio of their tanks or fighter aircraft to ours – as if to underscore our hopelessness in any future conflict. Next time, the briefers would tell us not to worry because most Soviet units would not even know where they were on the battlefield because the unit alcoholics would have drained all the fluid from their compasses.

Likewise, the intelligence analysts speculated that the non-Russian Soviet units would defect and refuse to fight when the first bullets were fired. It was all very confusing and, in retrospect, downright amusing, given the extremes. We assumed then, as we do now, that reality was somewhere in between those opposite poles.

When it comes to the transition from military to civilian careers, the messages for veterans today are equally bipolar, exaggerated, and inaccurate. A dispassionate observer might think that we have gone mad as a society when we cannot decide whether our veterans are losers or heroes.

Hollywood and the media would have us believe that our streets are teeming with roaming zombie-like hordes of chronically unemployable veterans. Rendered incapable by PTS and distracted daily by thoughts of depression, these veterans are thought to be employable only through the good faith and charity of philanthropic and patriotic corporate initiatives such as the Veterans Jobs Mission or the hundreds of variants on "hiring heroes."

At the other extreme, transition classes and word-of-mouth scuttlebutt can paint a rosy scenario in which companies are lined up outside the gates of military bases, eager to offer above-market compensation and risk-free training to transitioning servicemembers of all skills, abilities, and motivations. So the ambitious, determined veteran career seeker should be forgiven if he or she is confused.

The indisputable fact is that veterans are America's best talent. Companies are waking up to the reality that they need to compete to attract and retain the highest-quality veteran talent. Barriers and misinformation remain. It is up to the veteran to directly contradict the myths by word and deed.

You probably are not a hero

Are you as an honorable veteran worthy of respect and admiration for your service, competence, and dedication? Of course! Are you a hero? Perhaps, but probably not. Be that as it may, the label of hero will not help drive civilian success. If we use the word hero for every veteran, we lose the ability to describe those who achieve or sacrifice on the highest level. All veterans need to be proud of honorable service, but most of us do not rise to the level of hero.

Janet Jackson's lyric, "What have you done for me lately?" is the name of the game in the civilian world. Can you make, sell, or count stuff to create more value than you are paid? These are the key questions that employers will ask. Claiming – or not dismissing – the title of hero will do very little to answer these questions and will lull the veteran job seeker into inactivity, if taken too seriously.

But you are a winner

In the government and the non-profit sectors, resources are marshalled to address defined problems. Because of this law of political economics, the continued existence of many entities depends on the perpetuation of the veterans-as-victims narrative. This is not to dismiss the good intentions of most of these organizations, nor the true needs of certain individual veterans. Most of the people who work with veterans care deeply about their well-being. But you, as an individual veteran, must not view yourself as a victim.

No private employer can long survive by hiring low-quality employees. Winning organizations seek the best talent. That is where the true value of veterans comes to the fore. No other surviving part of our society teaches accountability and performance like the military.

Your veteran status says something significant about you. First, you volunteered. You ran to the sound of the guns when most others ignored the call. Then, because of your uniformed experiences, you became a better, more employable individual. Companies and other organizations will be lucky to have you on their teams.

Job seeking is a rollercoaster of emotions and experiences in the best of times. Do not compound the experience by listening to the two voices whispering in your ears – the voice of the angel who tells you that it will all be puppies and rainbows on the way to your dream job, or the voice of the demon with its message of defeatism and despair. Both are incorrect. Your search will be hard, arduous work, but if you know yourself and what you plan to accomplish, you will achieve your career goals.

The myth of job postings

Of all the many myths that attend the veteran job-search process, perhaps one of the most widespread is the belief that answering job postings online suffices for a comprehensive job-search strategy. It is very common for job seekers to spend hours every day firing off resumes and cover letters to every online posting to which they can rationalize some sort of a connection. Not surprisingly, these efforts usually fail to even elicit responses from the employers. This failure can breed frustration for the job seeker, leading to bouts of self-pity and defeatism.

It took only a few months into the evolution of the commercial Internet during the late 1990's for employment media companies to transform the old newspaper help wanted advertisement into the online job posting. At first, it seemed like a magical solution. From the comfort of the job seeker's computer, he could send resumes directly to employers in response to their stated needs. No longer would job seekers have to print their letters and credentials on fancy paper, lick stamps, and wait weeks for company responses.

Employers quickly discovered that the ease with which job seekers could apply resulted in an oversupply of candidates who often had only the most tenuous fit for the advertised opening. So the employers came to regard job postings as a necessary tool, but one that was fraught with inefficiencies of time, money, and efficacy. Job seekers learned that, in most cases, applying online was akin to firing communications into a virtual black hole of non-responsiveness.

CareerXroads estimates that today a mere 13.2% of jobs are found via online postings. So why do military-experienced job seekers continue to follow this path? Convenience. Given the choice between the intangible hard work of live networking and developing social networks versus sitting at home requesting LinkedIn connections and applying to jobs online, most will select the latter. And they will assume that the latter are sufficient. Following this course makes the job seekers feel as if they are "doing something," even though they are not working too hard or very intelligently. The strategy even has a name: spray and pray.

But rather than blindly apply to job postings online, in most cases veteran job seekers should see a company's posting primarily as a valuable piece of intelligence. It is critical to know that a company has (or perhaps until recently had) an open position. One should study the job description and articulate to oneself why the position is a fit for one's skills, ambitions, and experience.

If an online job catches the seeker's fancy, she must figure out how to get directly to the hiring managers for the position. Some techniques include calling the company and asking a receptionist who is responsible for hiring that position or leveraging LinkedIn to identify useful relationships. Like a military S-2 unit or a crime profiler, the veteran job seeker needs to summon his inner sleuth to find a way to identify the appropriate people. Ideally, the networking job seeker will learn of a position before it is posted. Remember that some postings exist only for regulatory or corporate diversity compliance. If you do not get in before the job is posted, you may be too late.

The key to effective job searching is to get referred by a person trusted by the employer. And veterans acquire such access through networking.

It bears mentioning that job postings tend to be more effective when the position calls for a very specific skill set. Job seekers who offer specific and recognized certifications that match the job need – for example, people such as registered nurses and programmers of certain software languages – will have better luck with direct posting applications than those with general skills and degrees.

Online postings are readily available to all job seekers. Used in conjunction with a focused networking strategy that includes quality career-fair attendance and truly bilateral conversations, postings are a valuable source of intelligence and insight – and occasionally direct access to jobs. Utilizing postings alone is akin to buying lottery tickets as the sole means of attaining financial independence. You might get lucky, but the odds are not with you.

Myths of education

In America, we believe that education is the key to getting ahead. Everyone is encouraged to finish high school. Many are urged to earn a college degree or technical certification.

On the whole, education is a good and worthy goal. But not all degrees and certifications are worth pursuing with equal vigor, and many are inappropriate for certain students. What with the "free" and generous nature of the Post-9/11 GI Bill, many veterans have a poor understanding of the real and opportunity costs of spending years pursuing degrees or certifications that neither match their best personal career paths or the needs of the marketplace.

Before consuming education during or after a transition from military service, one must understand exactly what he or she seeks from the investment and verify if there is indeed demand in the workplace for that credential.

There are four fundamental reasons to consume education as an adult:
- credential for professional access
- brand
- knowledge
- experience

Each individually and all collectively are valid reasons to return to school. By establishing and maintaining a clear and dispassionate understanding of these justifications before investing time and money, a veteran is likely to avoid the feelings of betrayal, frustration, and exploitation that attend some freshly-degreed job seekers who fail to realize much return on their investment.

Credential for professional access

In certain professions, one simply must have the appropriate degree to work. Medical doctors, dentists, accountants, registered nurses, home inspectors, and lawyers must have certifications and/or licenses to practice. So there can be no debate that one who wants to work in one of these professions must attend and complete the appropriate school.

But, especially in fields that require a lot of education, a would-be student should do extensive research before starting a school to determine whether she really wishes to work in that field and is a good temperamental fit.

For example, it is common to find an undergraduate struggling through an accounting degree program fueled by the general notion that "accountants will always have good jobs." A more accurate version of that adage would be "good accountants generally will find good jobs." An individual who is neither skilled at math nor well organized will make a poor accountant and should not set out on that degree path.

Furthermore, many professions like sales, entrepreneurship, and general business operations do not require any meaningful certifications or degrees. Programs may exist, but their completion is not a prerequisite for access or success. Be sure to do your research to learn the difference.

Brand

The institution that grants a certification or degree bestows its name on the student who graduates from its halls. Not all schools are equal. Most people know that only the best high school students apply to Harvard – and of those, only 5% are admitted – so people generally assume that a Harvard graduate must be, until proven otherwise, very smart and intellectually gifted. This is the power of a premier brand.

Other types of educational institutions bear different brands. Graduates of the military service academies, for example, are presumed to be disciplined and well-rounded.

Most institutions lack such cachet. The vast majority of colleges are not nearly as selective or elite as Ivy League universities or service academies. But even so, they do communicate something, rightly or wrongly, about their students. Before investing in a degree or certification, ask yourself and others what will possessing this degree say about me?

It should be noted that branding can come from the type of educational experience as well as the institution itself. For example, earning an executive MBA from a reputable program while holding a job and raising a family communicates time management and discipline on behalf of the candidate even if the institution is not particularly exclusive. But it does not communicate intellectual gifts if the program is not selective, nor does it necessarily impress employers. Understand your potential return on investment by really getting a sense of the brand value of your program.

Knowledge

It is amazing how many students start an educational program without considering fully what they will actually learn. Military instruction, incidentally, is highly disciplined about laying out learning objectives: "at the conclusion of this lesson, the student will be able to . . ." It is critical that you really understand the volume and quantity of knowledge to be transferred. What is the pedagogical philosophy of the school? Does it teach the way you learn best? What will you really be able to do that you cannot today?

Get beyond simplistic benefits like "I will be able to think more clearly" and define direct benefits such as "I will be able to perform financial analysis well enough to become a bank examiner or money manager."

Experience

A good education provides an experience in excess of the actual knowledge, brand, and credential. It may be the ability to interact with faculty and peers in a memorable or meaningful way. Perhaps it is the chance to meet future employers at school functions or partaking in extracurricular activities. All these are completely valid reasons to pursue an education program, but one must be mindful of what he seeks from each.

So when deciding whether to purchase an educational degree or certification, ask these critical questions:
- Is this certification or degree required for professional access to the career I seek? Am I well suited for this career? Have I tested the claims of school recruiters by talking to four or five hiring managers in the field regarding demand for graduates?
- What will the school brand offer me? Will it communicate something essential about me to the marketplace?
- What will I really learn that I could not learn elsewhere on my own?

- What about the school's student experience is unique, special, or particularly attractive?

If someone buys a car that is poorly reviewed in the automotive press, he has only himself to blame if he does not enjoy driving it. Adult consumers of education likewise are solely responsible for their own good decisions.

Truth be told, some veterans seek degrees and certifications because they, consciously or unconsciously, want to avoid having to make the serious and mature decision of what they really want to do with their careers. A significant portion of those who pursue degrees or certifications are procrastinating yet "doing something" to impress friends and family. The time to figure out what you want to do with your life and career is before – not after – you begin your course of study.

The right education for each person can make his life and career better. Poor and sloppy decisions waste years and resources that could be put to better use. It is not a school's fault if you fail to do your homework.

*"A hero is someone who has given his or her life
to something bigger than oneself."*

Joseph Campbell

Chapter 19
Veteran Success Stories

The greatest pleasure and honor that we experience at RecruitMilitary is the success stories that we collect from our veteran candidates. The following are just a small sample of the stories of these extraordinary people but regular veterans.

Camilla Hull
"I refused to be a statistic"

Army veteran encourages education, saying, "Civilians care nothing about you jumping out of a plane, but the letters behind your name hold weight."

Sergeant Camilla Gore Hull knew that joining the United States Army would prepare her for a brighter future. "I was a young, single parent and refused to be a statistic. I married the father of my child and joined the military to obtain funds for college and to gain work experience," she explained.

Her father retired from the Army, and Hull served for eight years from 1989 – 1997 as a surgical technician and an instructor of DepMed equipment. Her assignments took her to Belgium and Germany, and included a deployment with the 2nd MASH from Fort Benning as part of Operation Desert Shield/Storm. "The military taught me to believe in myself, to constantly set goals, and to never become complacent," Hull said.

One of the most valuable skills she learned during her service was becoming CPR trained at any early age. "It gave me a sense of responsibility and instilled in me the importance of continued education," she said.

When it came time for her to re-enter the civilian world, Hull turned to job fairs to hone in on a career. Her biggest challenge in looking for a civilian job was deciding exactly where she wanted to be. "But being a veteran provided me with a head start," she said. "Veterans possess a sense of loyalty. We make good employees; we are proficient in making decisions, have a strong work ethic, and are flexible."

Hull landed her current role as HSE Coordinator for Cummins Power South at a RecruitMilitary career fair in Atlanta. Today she handles worker's compensation claims, and provides safety training for employees while ensuring the company complies with OSHA regulations. "RecruitMilitary helped me in finding a career – not just a job," she said.

Veterans who are transitioning or seeking new careers can do several things to get ready, according to Hull:

- **Maximize your GI Bill benefits.** "Obtain as much education as you can with the GI Bill, so that your student loans will be decreased if you should choose to seek further education. I made the mistake of allowing mine to expire before I used them all, which caused me to pay out of pocket for my master's degree."

- **Sign up to learn.** This means taking advantage of any education and certification opportunities. "Civilians care nothing about you jumping out of a plane, but the letters behind your name hold weight."

- **Give your resume a revamp.** "Use professionals that are proficient in preparing them for veterans."

- **Hit the fairs.** "Career fairs may seem overwhelming. Believe in yourself, and attend them prepared for an on-site interview," she encouraged.

Larry Enriquez
Elevated by Education

*How one soldier's journey took him
all the way from Army Reserve Specialist
to becoming a commissioned officer*

Larry Enriquez's reasons for joining the military were simple and pure. "I truly wanted to serve my country. I grew up in the U.S. with so much opportunity, and I wanted to give back." Although his grandfather served in the Navy, he is the first in his immediate family to serve.

A native of Bellingham, Washington and a successful long distance runner in high school, Enriquez wanted to continue running in college. The Army Reserve allowed him to do both, and he spent his freshman year at Highline Community College in the Seattle area on the track and field team. "I loved it and had a blast. It gave me a chance to travel all over and compete with other teams all the way up to Division 1."

The Army Reserve provided the tuition assistance that he needed. "Growing up, my family did not have a lot of money. I could not have gone to college without that," he said.

He acknowledged that managing school and the Reserve was challenging at times, as his annual training requirements took him out of the classroom and occasionally overseas. "But I made arrangements with my professors to take tests early and make up work, and they were always very understanding and accommodating," he said.

His schooling was interrupted for a year when he deployed to Baghdad in 2003 as part of Operation Iraqi Freedom. "My unit arrived right after Baghdad fell. At the time, we had no idea how long the conflict would last. We thought we'd be going home as soon as the new government was in place, but it turned into one year. Once I was even permitted to be in the war room with intelligence information coming in, because I had a security clearance."

Enriquez leveraged the Internet to take advantage of online coursework during his deployment. As a transportation and logistics specialist, he tracked and coordinated cargo and troops moving through the Baghdad airport, which had been converted to into a large base occupied by coalition forces. A few months after arriving in Iraq, the insurgency began periodically launching mortar and rocket rounds onto the base. After running to the bunkers for safety the first few times, he and his fellow soldiers gradually got used to their sound. He once witnessed a compound building explode close to where he was working in a nearby pallet yard. "At first I stood there in awe, but then I got right back to work," he said.

Occasionally he would interact with local Iraqi children when his job took him through the slums of Baghdad to check on railroad cargo. "The kids thought we were superheroes with all the gear that we had, and they asked lots of questions. They were mostly little boys, anywhere from seven to nine years old," he recalled. "We would bring them candy and we played soccer with them wearing all our gear, and they always beat us."

Upon returning stateside, Enriquez was anxious to finish up his associate's degree and move on to Western Washington University (WWU) in Bellingham to earn a bachelor's degree in business management. "Having been deployed, I felt I had a better understanding of what was going on in Iraq than other, more opinionated students," he said, "but I avoided getting into any arguments about it."

Although the veteran community in Bellingham and at WWU was not large, Enriquez interacted closely with the VA office on campus that coordinated his tuition benefits, something he advises other veterans to do as well. "Take advantage of that office. They will help you," he said.

After graduating in 2007, Enriquez headed to the warmer climate of Huntington Beach, California and joined the corporate world as a recruiter at a staffing firm. That experience quickly helped him realize that he really wanted to pursue a career in law enforcement. Knowing that landing a job in California was highly competitive, he gained experience by working at a private security firm with the goal of becoming a police officer. "I decided I wanted to be in a profession that allowed me to give back, just like I had done in the Army," he said. "I wanted to be part of something that was bigger than myself."

While working in private security, Enriquez began considering returning to the Army once he'd earned his bachelor's degree. "I talked to a recruiter and asked if he could get me into officer candidate school (OCS). It's a very competitive process: it took me six months to put together my packet of essays, work experience, and letters of recommendation. Then I had to appear before a board and go through a series of grueling interviews, but it all worked out because I passed," he said.

Enriquez found himself in the unique position of going through basic training again, this time at Fort Benning, Georgia. "At 32, I was the old guy among 18- and 19-year olds. But because I'd always kept physically fit, I beat a lot of them in activities like running and pushups. When I finished, my drill instructor drove me over to the other side of Fort Benning to begin officer candidate school."

"I'd been told that OCS was like basic training on steroids, and it was definitely the most challenging school I've ever been to. About 25% of the candidates don't make it through on the first try," he said.

With more academic responsibilities, including reading, research, and presentations, Enriquez drew upon the skills the Army taught him as an enlisted soldier. "I had already learned to be humble and be thick-skinned, so that helped me not to take any criticism personally. I was able to just learn from it and move on."

Networking with other young officers beforehand helped, too. "They really set my expectations going in, and gave me advice about courses and other challenges I'd be encountering." He graduated from OCS in November of 2014 with lots of family in attendance.

The next step toward achieving his goal: military police (MP) school at Fort Leonard Wood, Missouri. "I loved the field exercises and hands-on stuff the best. I also had to do a lot of public speaking. We'd receive make-believe battle scenarios and present our plan for how to resolve various situations."

Enriquez also received training on active shooter scenarios, patrolling, clearing buildings, and firing weapons ranging from handguns to belt-fed automatic machine guns. Part of the rigorous program included being tazed and sprayed with pepper spray, which he described as "like someone putting a blow torch on your face."

"Aside from funding my education, the military taught me to be organized and to plan ahead. I'm still a work in progress, but I'm much more efficient with my time now," he said.

Steven Bartimus
From Garage Band to Global Operations

*Fateful Internet search led former
Marine infantry NCO to RecruitMilitary
and to his second career.*

Steven Bartimus's path to the military might be categorized as the road less taken. The Alabama native was working toward a degree in music and was already started on a career path doing hazardous industrial sand blasting and painting when he decided to join up. "I was a garage band guitarist from the 90's, but I was restless. I was trying to find a challenge in life," he explained.

From Rocker to Marine

Becoming a Marine appealed to him as a true test in both physical and mental dexterity and endurance. Upon entering the USMC recruiting office with long hair, "The recruiter took one look at me and said, 'Where's the clippers?'"

Bartimus told the recruiters that he wanted to serve in RECON and the infantry, one of the most difficult specialties available in the Marine Corps, and the foundation of the Marine Corps. "Infantrymen are trained to locate, close with, and destroy the enemy by fire and maneuver, or repel the enemy's assault by fire and close combat," he said.

"Once they realized I was serious, I filled out the application and was off to MEPS (Military Entrance Processing Station). Pretty soon after that I was a 25-year old in boot camp at Parris Island. My nickname was 'Grandpa,'" he said. He noted, "I requested to be part of the most difficult battalion on Parris Island, the 3rd Battalion, and luckily I assigned there."

Boot camp taught Bartimus how to be part of a team, and how to support his fellow Marines. "I also learned that your team is only as strong as your weakest link. It sounds corny, but it's true: there is no 'I' in 'team.'"

A Fateful Encounter
Upon entering the Fleet Marine Forces, he deployed to the Mediterranean Ocean and Adriatic Sea with the 24th MEU (Marine Expeditionary Unit) just before the war in Kosovo in 1999. His unit was staged to take control of and occupy the Pristina Airport. The United Nations and Coalition Forces were to use this base as a hub for supplies. "None of us knew the big picture as to why we were going in – but we knew what we were up against and we were ready to execute our mission."

Bartimus moved on to assignments in Japan and got out of the Marines right before 9/11. He was working as a contractor supporting the Army when a fateful Internet search led him to RecruitMilitary. He completed his candidate profile on the company's website. The same day a RecruitMilitary recruiter contacted him, ultimately leading to a placement with Titan Corporation, a defense contractor.

He then deployed to the western region of Iraq, Al Anbar Province, and worked as a site manager for linguists and translators at Al Asad Air Base. "I managed mostly locally hired linguists and I had to make sure they were paid and taken care of. There were no banks, and no direct deposit options available, so I had a big bag of cash on me at all times. I'd drive around, find the linguists and pay them," he said.

He rose quickly within the company and became a program manager. Bartimus went on to work with other defense contractors in the linguist support arena, including Mission Essential managing OCONUS operations in the United Kingdom, Germany, Italy, Northern Iraq, the Horn of Africa, and Afghanistan.

Bartimus's business travels brought him to Kosovo once again in 2008. While touring historic sites in the village of Perka, he saw a monument memorializing the struggle of the ethnic Albanian people and the Jasharis family, who formed a resistance force against ethnic oppression. The family's fatal last stand against Slobodan Milosevic's forces received international attention and led to UN and Coalition involvement in the region.

While viewing the historic sights and talking with remaining members of the Jasharis family, Bartimus soon realized they were the reason his USMC unit had been sent there ten years earlier to assist in resolving that conflict. "The story came full circle, and I shared my experience with my fellow Marines who had been there with me ten years earlier," he said.

Investing in People

Bartimus continued to ascend in the ranks at Mission Essential, becoming a senior program manager as the company expanded into Afghanistan. He oversaw more than 8,000 linguists and 200 deployed staff. To this day, he credits his success to the leadership and management skills he learned in the Marines. "It instilled in me how to understand people. Show people you actually care about their world. Get in the trenches with your personnel and work side by side. Once people see that, you will gain their respect and they will follow you."

Building positive relationships is something Bartimus believes is often missing in Corporate America. "Companies have to stop solely focusing on the numbers, and start thinking about people. Yes, it's a business, but if companies take care of the people working for them, they will remain loyal and outperform all expectations. But, it must really be embraced at the top and truly become part of the culture," he said.

Bartimus now works in Washington, D.C. as a government contractor and consultant to DoD contractors. "RecruitMilitary led me to an opportunity to build a successful life with unimaginable experiences. I can't wait to see what the future has in store," he said.

Jeff Garner
The Art of Spinning

*Air Force veteran applied old skills
to launch new career*

When Jeff Garner decided to retire rather quickly from the Air Force after 20 years of service, he admittedly had little time to prepare for a civilian job search. The Air Force Master Sergeant (E-7) and 20-year veteran had extensive experience working with fuels and aircraft and had served in England, Guam, Nevada, and Germany before retiring and heading to Phoenix.

Although he had also earned a master's degree in human resources, and had gained HR experience as a first sergeant, Garner aimed to return to the fuel industry. However, he knew getting back to that field would be difficult, so he began considering the water industry as an alternative. Garner attended a RecruitMilitary hiring event and connected with a water company, EPCOR. HR representatives were on site and took his resume, which led to an online application and an interview the following week. He began working in March 2015 as a water system plant operator. "I hit the bullseye," he said.

Garner's favorite thing about the service was the people he worked alongside as well as being part of a team. He deployed nine days after 9/11 to Spain to assist with the buildup to go into Afghanistan. He is also grateful for the technical skills he learned, and the opportunities for education and advancement; he earned two associate's degrees, a bachelor's degree in management, and a master's degree in human resources. "Overall, the military teaches you so much you don't realize you have," he said.

"My military career gave me so many directions I could've gone in: OSHA training, FEMA, lab work, HR work...that's something I'm grateful for," he remarked.

"Vets have so much to offer," Garner said. "Our leadership experience and training, our dedication and loyalty. Whether you serve four or 20 years, you develop the skills of being on time, having integrity and doing the right thing."

Garner offers this advice to veterans who are seeking new careers:

■ Social media is a great place to connect, but face-to-face interaction is the best, and career fairs offer invaluable platforms to meet potential employers.

■ Think outside the box, and learn to break down your transferable skills. Just because you have a background in ammunition, be open-minded about where that can take you.

- Learn how to spin: "Even though I was interviewing for a position with a water company and my experience was in fuels, I did know about safety and how to test jet fuels, so I spun that and talked it up."

"Seeking a new career forced me to examine my skills and experience and see where else they could apply. I was able to spin my old skills into a new career," Garner said.

*"Simple can be harder than complex:
You have to work hard to get
your thinking clean to make it simple.
But it's worth it in the end
because once you get there,
you can move mountains."*

Steve Jobs

Appendix

Conclusion

Veterans truly represent the finest talent our country has to offer. Organizations of all stripes thrive when they include veteran hiring initiatives among their best conceived and executed human resource strategies.

Hiring veterans is not hard. To be sure, it is a task and strategy that requires effort, resources, and resilience. The return on that investment, however, is massive. Furthermore, you will never be alone in this endeavor. There are 22 million veterans in this country, 10 million of whom are active in the workforce. Almost all of these fine Americans stand by to assist you with wisdom, connections, and time.

Remember, as you follow the advice of this handbook, do not sweat the small stuff. If your heart is in the right place, good outcomes will follow. Whereas there is a right and wrong way to recruit veterans for maximum effect, we need to follow the sage advice of the band 38 Special and "hold on loosely but don't let go."

Table A

Types of Enlisted Personnel

The following are examples of types of occupations for enlisted personnel. This table is taken from the Bureau of Labor Statistics.[18]

Administrative personnel maintain information on personnel, equipment, funds, and other military-related activities. They work in support areas, such as finance, accounting, legal affairs, maintenance, supply, and transportation.

Combat specialty personnel train and work in combat units, such as the infantry, artillery, or special forces. For example, infantry specialists conduct ground combat operations, armored vehicle specialists operate battle tanks, and seamanship specialists maintain ships. Combat specialty personnel may maneuver against enemy forces and fire artillery, guns, mortars, or missiles to neutralize them. They may also operate various types of combat vehicles, such as amphibious assault vehicles, tanks, or small boats. Members of elite Special Forces teams are trained to perform specialized missions anywhere in the world on a moment's notice.

18

http://www.bls.gov/ooh/military/military-careers.htm

Construction personnel build or repair buildings, airfields, bridges, and other structures. They may also operate heavy equipment, such as bulldozers or cranes. They work with engineers and other building specialists as part of military construction teams. Some construction personnel specialize in an area such as plumbing, electrical wiring, or water purification.

Electronic and electrical equipment repair personnel maintain and repair electronic equipment used by the military. Repairers specialize in an area such as aircraft electrical systems, computers, optical equipment, communications, or weapons systems. For example, weapons electronic maintenance technicians maintain and repair electronic components and systems that help locate targets and help aim and fire weapons.

Engineering, science, and technical personnel perform a variety of tasks, such as operating technical equipment, solving problems, and collecting and interpreting information. They perform technical tasks in information technology, environmental health and safety, or intelligence:

- Information technology specialists manage and maintain computer and network systems.
- Environmental health and safety specialists inspect military facilities and food supplies to ensure that they are safe for use and consumption.
- Intelligence specialists gather information and prepare reports for military planning and operations.

Healthcare personnel provide medical services to military personnel and their family members. They may work as part of a patient-service team with doctors, nurses, or other healthcare professionals. Some specialize in providing emergency medical treatment in combat or remote areas. Others specialize in laboratory testing of tissue and blood samples; maintaining pharmacy supplies or patients' records; assisting with dental procedures; operating diagnostic tools, such as x-ray and ultrasound machines; or other healthcare tasks.

Human resources development personnel recruit qualified people into the military, place them in suitable occupations, and provide training programs:

- Personnel specialists maintain information about military personnel and their training, job assignments, promotions, and health.
- Recruiting specialists provide information about military careers; explain pay, benefits, and military life; and recruit individuals into the military.
- Training specialists and instructors teach military personnel how to perform their jobs.

Machine operator and repair personnel operate industrial equipment and machinery to make and repair parts for a variety of equipment and structures. They may operate engines, nuclear reactors, or water pumps, usually performing a specific job. Welders and metalworkers, for example, work with various types of metals to repair or form the structural parts of ships, buildings, or equipment. Survival equipment specialists inspect, maintain, and repair survival equipment, such as parachutes and aircraft life-support equipment.

Media and public affairs personnel prepare and present information about military activities to the military and the public. They take photographs, make video programs, present news and music programs, or conduct interviews.

Protective service personnel enforce military laws and regulations and provide emergency responses to disasters:
- Firefighters prevent and extinguish fires in buildings, on aircraft, and aboard ships.
- Military police responsibilities include controlling traffic, preventing crime, and responding to emergencies.
- Other law enforcement and security specialists investigate crimes committed on military property and guard inmates in military correctional facilities.

Support service personnel provide services that support the morale and well-being of military personnel and their families:
- Food service specialists prepare food in dining halls, hospitals, and ships.
- Religious program specialists assist chaplains with religious services, religious education programs, and related administrative duties.

Transportation and material-handling personnel transport military personnel and cargo. Most personnel within this occupational group are classified according to the mode of transportation, such as aircraft, motor vehicle, or ship:

- Aircrew members operate equipment on aircraft.
- Cargo specialists load and unload military supplies, using forklifts and cranes.
- Quartermasters and boat operators navigate and pilot many types of small watercraft, including tugboats, gunboats, and barges.
- Vehicle drivers operate various military vehicles, including fuel or water tank trucks.

Vehicle and machinery mechanical personnel conduct preventive and corrective maintenance on aircraft, automotive and heavy equipment, and powerhouse station equipment. These workers specialize by the type of equipment that they maintain:

- Aircraft mechanics inspect and service various types of aircraft.
- Automotive and heavy-equipment mechanics maintain and repair vehicles, such as Humvees, trucks, tanks, and other combat vehicles. They also repair bulldozers and other construction equipment.
- Heating and cooling mechanics install and repair air-conditioning, refrigeration, and heating equipment.
- Marine engine mechanics repair and maintain engines on ships, boats, and other watercraft.
- Powerhouse mechanics install, maintain, and repair electrical and mechanical equipment in power-generating stations.

Table B

Types of Officer Roles

Combat specialty officers plan and direct military operations, oversee combat activities, and serve as combat leaders. They may be in charge of tanks and other armored assault vehicles, artillery systems, special operations, or infantry units. This group also includes naval surface warfare and submarine warfare officers, combat pilots, and aircrews.

Engineering, science, and technical officers' responsibilities depend on their area of expertise. They work in scientific and professional occupations, such as atmospheric scientists, meteorologists, physical scientists, biological scientists, social scientists, attorneys, and other types of scientists or professionals. For example, meteorologists in the military may study the weather to assist in planning flight paths for aircraft.

Executive, administrative, and managerial officers manage administrative functions in the Armed Forces, such as human resources management, training, personnel, information, police, or other support services. Officers who oversee military bands are included in this category.

Healthcare officers provide medical services to military personnel in order to maintain or improve their health and physical readiness. Officers such as physicians, physician assistants, nurses, and dentists examine, diagnose, and treat patients. Other healthcare officers provide therapy, rehabilitative treatment, and additional healthcare for patients:

- Dentists treat diseases, disorders, and injuries of the mouth.
- Nurses provide and coordinate patient care in military hospitals and clinics.
- Optometrists treat vision problems and prescribe glasses, contact lenses, or medications.
- Pharmacists purchase, store, and dispense drugs and medicines.
- Physical therapists and occupational therapists plan and administer therapy to help patients adjust to injuries, regain independence, and return to work.
- Physicians, surgeons, and physician assistants examine patients, diagnose injuries and illnesses, and provide treatment to military and their families.
- Psychologists provide mental healthcare and may also conduct research on behavior and emotions.

Human resource development officers manage recruitment, placement, and training programs in the military:

- Personnel managers direct and oversee military personnel functions, such as job assignments, staff promotions, and career counseling.
- Recruiting managers direct and oversee recruiting personnel and recruiting activities.

- Training and education directors identify training needs and develop and manage educational programs.

Media and public affairs officers oversee the development, production, and presentation of information or events for the military and the public. They manage the production of videos and television and radio broadcasts that are used for training, news, and entertainment. Some plan, develop, and direct the activities of military bands. Public affairs officers respond to public inquiries about military activities and prepare news releases.

Protective service officers are responsible for the safety and protection of individuals and property on military bases and vessels. Emergency management officers plan and prepare for all types of disasters. They develop warning, evacuation, and response procedures in preparation for disasters. Law enforcement and security officers enforce all applicable laws on military bases and oversee investigations of crimes.

Support services officers manage military activities in key functional areas, such as logistics, transportation, and supply. They may oversee the transportation and distribution of materials by ground vehicles, aircraft, or ships. They also direct food service facilities and other support activities. Purchasing and contracting managers negotiate and monitor contracts for equipment, supplies, and services that the military buys from the private sector.

Transportation officers manage and perform activities related to the safe transport of military personnel and equipment by air and water. They operate and command an aircraft or a ship:

- Navigators use radar, radio, and other navigation equipment to determine their position and plan their route of travel.
- Pilots in the military fly various types of military airplanes and helicopters to carry troops and equipment.
- Ships' engineers direct engineering departments, including engine operations, maintenance, and power generation, aboard ships.

Glossary of Military Terms

═ ⋆ ★ ⋆ ═

Access to Classified Information	The ability and opportunity to obtain knowledge of classified information by persons with the proper security clearance and a need to know of specified classified information.
Active Duty	Full-time duty in the active military service of the United States, including active duty or full-time training duty in the Reserve Component. Also called AD.
Active Guard and Reserve	National Guard and Reserve members who are on voluntary active duty providing full-time support to National Guard, Reserve, and Active Component organizations for the purpose of organizing, administering, recruiting, instructing, or training the Reserve Components.
Administrative Chain of Command	One of the two branches of the chain of command described in Joint Publication 1, Doctrine for the Armed Forces of the United States, through which command is exercised from the President through the Secretary of Defense to the Secretaries of the Military Departments, and from which forces are assigned to combatant commands to compose the operational command structure baseline.

Glossary of Military Terms
=＝ ∗ ⭐ ∗ ＝

Administrative Contracting Officer	Contracting officer whose primary duties involve contract administration.
Administrative Plan or Order	A combat plan or order relating to the operation plan or order for a tactical operation. It sets forth information and instructions governing the logistical and administrative support of the operation.
Air and Missile Defense	Direct [active and passive] defensive actions taken to destroy, nullify, or reduce the effectiveness of hostile air and ballistic missile threats against friendly forces and assets.
Airborne	1. In relation to personnel, troops especially trained to effect, following transport by air, an assault debarkation, either by parachuting or touchdown. 2. In relation to equipment, pieces of equipment that have been especially designed for use by airborne troops during or after an assault debarkation as well as some aeronautical equipment used to accomplish a particular mission. 3. When applied to materiel, items that form an integral part of the aircraft. 4. The state of an aircraft, from the instant it becomes entirely sustained by air until it ceases to be so sustained.

Glossary of Military Terms

=★ ★ ★=

Aircraft Carrier	A warship designed to support and operate aircraft, engage in attacks on targets afloat or ashore, and engage in sustained operations in support of other forces. Also called CV or CVN.
Air Defense	Defensive measures designed to destroy attacking enemy aircraft or missiles in the atmosphere, or to nullify or reduce the effectiveness of such attack. Also called AD.
Air Liaison Officer	The senior tactical air control party member attached to a ground unit who functions as the primary advisor to the ground commander on air power. Also called ALO.
Area Command	A command that is composed of elements of one or more of the Services, organized and placed under a single commander and designated to operate in a specific geographical area.

Glossary of Military Terms

=== ★ ★ ===

Bang-bang	An Army term describing a pistol or rifle.
Battalion Forward Defense Area	Portion of a battle area defended by front-line companies; it extends to the limit of the rearward extension of lateral boundaries of the front-line companies.
Bird	Slang for helicopter.
Carrier Air Wing	Two or more aircraft squadrons formed under one commander for administrative and tactical control of operations from a carrier. Also called CVW.
Chain of Command	The succession of commanding officers from a superior to a subordinate through which command is exercised. Also called command channel.
Checkpoint	An easily identifiable point on the terrain that is used in controlling movement or reporting locations of friendly units.
Chest Candy	Slang for ribbons and medals worn on a uniform.

Glossary of Military Terms

=★★=

Close Air Support	Air operations against the enemy executed at very close range to friendly front lines.
Collection Agency	Any individual, organization, or unit that has access to sources of information and the capability of collecting information from them.
Combat Engineering	Engineering capabilities and activities that directly support the maneuver of land combat forces that require close and integrated support. Basically building things and blowing things up.
Combat Information Center	The agency in a ship or aircraft manned and equipped to collect, display, evaluate, and disseminate tactical information for the use of the embarked flag officer, commanding officer, and certain control agencies. Also called CIC.
Combat Order	An order issued by a commander for a combat operation specifying time and date of execution.

Glossary of Military Terms

=== ★ ===

Combat Patrol	A patrol whose primary mission is to engage actively in combat with the enemy and whose secondary mission is to gain information about the enemy and the terrain.
Command and Control	The exercise of authority and direction by a properly designated commander over assigned and attached forces in the accomplishment of the mission.
Command Post (CP)	The location of a unit's headquarters from which the commander and the staff operate.
CommO	Communications equipment or the individuals who operate it. Usually given to Communicators Officers on U.S. Navy vessels.
Communications Center	An agency that is responsible for the receipt, transmission, and delivery of messages.

Glossary of Military Terms

=★★=

Communications Security	The protection by all measures to deny access to unauthorized information of value that might be derived from a study or receipt of communications.
Covert Operations	Operations that are so planned and executed as to conceal the identity of the sponsor.
Debarkation	The unloading of troops, equipment, or supplies from a ship or aircraft.
Delayed Entry Program	A program under which an individual may enlist in a Reserve Component of a military service and specify a future reporting date for entry on active duty that would coincide with availability of training spaces and with personal plans such as high school graduation. Also called DEP.
Deployment	The rotation of forces into and out of an operational area.

Glossary of Military Terms

=== ★ ★ ★ ===

Dittybopper	A term in the Army referring to signals intelligence radio operators trained to utilize Morse Code. Also used as a verb to describe soldiers marching out of synch with a cadence.
Double Time	Cadence at 180 steps (36 inches in length) per minute.
Dump	An area used for the temporary storage and disbursing of military supplies.
Eagle Keeper	Maintenance crew chief of an F-15.
Field Artillery	Equipment, supplies, ammunition, and personnel involved in the use of cannon, rocket, or surface-to-surface missile launchers. Also called FA.
Fire Direction Center	The element of a command post, consisting of gunnery and communication personnel and equipment, by means of which the commander exercises fire direction and fire control.

Glossary of Military Terms

═ ⋆ ★ ⋆ ═

Fire Support Team	Field artillery team provided for each maneuver company/troop and selected units to plan and coordinate all supporting fires available to the unit, including mortars, field artillery, naval surface fire support, and close air support integration. Also called FST.
Fire Support Officer	The field artillery officer from the operational to tactical level responsible for advising the supported commander or assisting the senior fires officer of the organization on fires functions and fire support. Also called FSO (or FO in the Marines).
Flank Guard	A security detachment that protects the flank of a body of troops on the march.
Flight Deck Officer	Officer responsible for the safe movement of aircraft on or about the flight deck of an aviation-capable ship. Also called FDO.
Formation	Arrangement of the elements of a unit in line, in column, or in any other prescribed manner.

Glossary of Military Terms

=★★=

Forward Air Controller (Airborne)	A specifically trained and qualified aviation officer, normally an airborne extension of the tactical air control party, who exercises control from the air of aircraft engaged in close air support of ground troops. Also called FAC(A).
Forward Observer	An observer operating with front line troops trained to adjust ground or naval gunfire and pass back battle-field information. Also called FO.
Fruit Salad	Slang for a service member's display of medals and ribbons on a dress uniform.
Gunner	A service member who operates a crew-served weapon, such as a piece of artillery or ship's cannon.
Human Intelligence	A category of intelligence derived from information collected and pro-vided by human sources. Also called HUMINT.

Glossary of Military Terms

=·★·=

Inventory Control	That phase of military logistics that includes managing, cataloging, requirements determinations, procurement, distribution, overhaul, and disposal of materiel. Also called inventory management; materiel control; materiel management; supply management.
Joint Operation Planning	All types of planning involving joint military forces in regard to military operations including, but not limited to, mobilization, deployment, and sustainment.
Landing Signalman Enlisted	Enlisted man responsible for ensuring that helicopters/tiltrotor aircraft, on signal, are safely started, engaged, launched, recovered, and shut down. Also called LSE.
Landing Signals Officer	Officer responsible for the visual control of aircraft in the terminal phase of the approach immediately prior to landing. Also called LSO.

Glossary of Military Terms

=== ⋆ ★ ⋆ ===

Logistic Support	Support that encompasses the logistic services, materiel, and transportation required to support the continental United States-based and worldwide deployed forces.
Maintenance	1. All action, including inspection, testing, servicing, classification as to serviceability, repair, rebuilding, and reclamation, taken to retain materiel in a serviceable condition or to restore it to serviceability. 2. All supply and repair action taken to keep a force in condition to carry out its mission. 3. The routine recurring work required to keep a facility in such condition that it may be continuously used at its original or designed capacity and efficiency for its intended purpose.
Manpower Management	The means of manpower control to ensure the most efficient and economical use of available manpower.
Marine Air Command and Control System	A system that provides the aviation combat element commander with the means to command, coordinate, and control all air operations within an assigned sector and to coordinate air operations with other Services. Also called MACCS.

Glossary of Military Terms

$=\star\bigstar\star=$

Materiel Planning	A subset of logistic planning consisting of the four-step process of: 1) Requirements definition. Requirements for significant items are calculated at item-level detail to support sustainability planning and analysis. 2) Apportionment. Items are apportioned to the combatant commanders based on a global scenario to avoid sourcing of items to multiple theaters. 3) Sourcing. Sourcing is the matching of available capabilities on a given date against item requirements to support sustainability analysis and the identification of locations to support transportation planning. 4) Documentation. Sourced item requirements are translated into movement requirements and documented in the Joint Operation Planning and Execution System database for transportation feasibility analysis.
Media Operations Center	A facility established by the commander to serve as the focal point for the interface between the military and the media during the conduct of military operations. Also called MOC.

Glossary of Military Terms

$=\!\cdot\!\bigstar\!\cdot\!=$

Military Sealift Command	A major command of the United States Navy reporting to Commander Fleet Forces Command, and the United States Transportation Command's component command responsible for designated common-user sealift transportation services to deploy, employ, sustain, and redeploy United States forces on a global basis. Also called MSC.
Mission	The specific task or duty assigned to an individual, weapon, or unit.
Officer of the Deck	Any officer charged with the operation of a ship. Reports to the commanding officer, executive officer, and navigator for relevant issues and concerns.
Operational Readiness	The capability of a unit/formation, ship, weapon system, or equipment to perform the missions or functions for which it is organized or designed. Also called OR.

Glossary of Military Terms

=★=

Operations Plan or Order	A combat plan or order dealing with tactical operations and setting forth the mission of the unit; it deals with the commander's decision, plan of action, and such details as to the method of execution as will ensure coordinated action by the whole command.
Patrol	A detachment sent out by a larger unit for the purpose of gathering information or carrying out a destructive, harassing, mop up, or security mission.
Rangers	Rapidly deployable airborne light infantry organized and trained to conduct highly complex joint direct action operations in coordination with or in support of other special operations units of all Services.
Rank	A line of men or vehicles placed side by side; officer's grade or position.

Glossary of Military Terms
═ ⋆ ★ ⋆ ═

Reconnaissance	A mission undertaken to obtain, by visual observation or other detection methods, information about the activities and resources of an enemy or adversary, or to secure data concerning the meteorological, hydrographic, or geographic characteristics of a particular area. Also called RECON.
Reconnaissance Patrol	A patrol whose mission is to gain information about the enemy and the terrain.
Red Team	A body of experts on a specific topic who are instructed to research and suggest alternative methods regarding a planned course of action.
Section	A military unit that is smaller than a platoon and larger than a squad; the basic tactical unit in the weapons platoon of the rifle company.

Glossary of Military Terms

=⋆★⋆=

Sensitive Compartmented Information	All information and materials bearing special community controls indicating restricted handling within present and future community intelligence collection programs and their end products for which community systems of compartmentation have been or will be formally established. (These controls are over and above the provisions of DOD 5200.1-R, Information Security Program Regulation.) Also called SCI.
Signals Intelligence	1. A category of intelligence comprising either individually or in combination all communications intelligence, electronic intelligence, and foreign instrumentation signals intelligence, however transmitted. 2. Intelligence derived from communications, electronic, and foreign instrumentation signals. Also called SIGINT.
SitRep	A situation report.
Special Operations Forces	Those Active and Reserve Component forces of the Services designated by the Secretary of Defense and specifically organized, trained, and equipped to conduct and support special operations. Also called SOF.

Glossary of Military Terms
═ ＊ ★ ＊ ═

Squadron	1. An organization consisting of two or more divisions of ships, or two or more divisions (Navy) or flights of aircraft. 2. The basic administrative aviation unit of the Army, Navy, Marine Corps, and Air Force. 3. Battalion-sized ground or aviation units.
Supply Point	A point where supplies are issued (for example, depot, railhead, truckhead, airhead).
Traffic Management	The direction, control, and supervision of all functions incident to the procurement and use of freight and passenger transportation services.
Unit	Any military force having a prescribed organization.
ZULU Time	A measure of time that conforms, within a close approximation, to the mean diurnal rotation of the Earth and serves as the basis of civil timekeeping. Also called Universal or Greenwich Mean Time.

References

Margaret C. Harrell and Nancy Berglass, "Employing America's Veterans: Perspectives from Business" (Center for a New American Security, June 2012)

Unpacking OFCCP's Final Rules for Veterans and Individuals with Disabilities. http://www.cooley.com/unpacking-OFCCPs-final-rules-for-veterans-and-individuals-with-disabilities

U.S. Department of Labor: general resources. http://www.dol.gov/dol/topic/hiring/veterans.htm

Harvard Business Review, November 2010. *"Which of These People Is Your Future CEO?: The Different Ways Military Experience Prepares Managers for Leadership"*

Acknowledgements

This handbook is the work of a team of dedicated professionals at RecruitMilitary. I am indebted to the insight and counsel of the following: Jay Myers, Elizabeth Stetler, Katie Becker, Linda Walters, Chris Cravens, Mike Francomb, Larry Slagel, and others.

We at RecruitMilitary are also indebted to our 2,500+ employer clients who show their intelligence everyday by hiring America's best talent, its veterans.

Finally, but primarily, I thank those who serve and have served. They are the special ones to whom the nation owes everything.

About RecruitMilitary

RecruitMilitary helps organizations excel by leveraging the talents of our nation's finest people, its military veterans. Specifically, the company helps employers, franchisors, and educational institutions attract, appreciate, and retain high-quality veteran talent.

RecruitMilitary's hiring services are free to men and women of all ranks/rates and all branches of the service who are transitioning from active duty to civilian life, veterans who already have civilian work experience, members of the National Guard and reserves, and military spouses and other family members.

RecruitMilitary produces career fairs for veteran job seekers throughout the United States; operates a job board and a database of more than 850,000 registered job seekers at www.recruitmilitary.com; conducts direct recruiting; publishes *Search & Employ*®, a bimonthly print and digital magazine with a print circulation of more than 45,000; emails a monthly jobs newsletter called *The VetTen*; provides targeted email marketing services; and maintains a website that carries links to employers' sites and careers pages.

All of RecruitMilitary's senior officers and most of its other employees have served in the armed forces. The company was founded in 1998 and is headquartered in Loveland, Ohio, near Cincinnati.

About the Author

Peter A. Gudmundsson is chief executive officer and president of Recruit-Military and a former artillery, infantry, and intelligence officer in the U.S. Marine Corps. Before purchasing RecruitMilitary in 2013, he served as CEO of the Dropout & Truancy Prevention Network, which combined technology with mentoring to keep students in school; founded the Priceless Legacy Company, which helped people preserve their life stories and lessons; was CEO and president of Beckett Media, publisher of magazines, books, and websites for sports collectors and gamers; founded and operated Design Guide Publishing, publisher of high-end interior design publications in three Texas cities; and served as president and CEO of Jobs.com, an Internet employment media company.

Before that, he was president of Primedia Workplace Learning, producer of online training media; vice president of Primedia Inc.; assistant to the president of Tosco Corporation; and an investment banker at Morgan Stanley & Company.

Gudmundsson is a graduate of Harvard Business School (MBA) and Brown University (BA, History). He currently serves as a volunteer officer in the Maritime Regiment of the Texas State Guard. Gudmundsson is married to the former Kathleen Vouté of Bronxville, New York. They have four children and live in Dallas.

RECRUIT//ILITARY®

RecruitMilitary exists to help organizations excel
by leveraging the talents of its best people, its veterans.

Specifically, RecruitMilitary helps employers,
franchisors, and educators attract, appreciate,
and retain high-quality veteran talent.

www.RecruitMilitary.com
513.683.5020